The Analytic Life

The Analytic Life

Personal and Professional Aspects
of Being
A Jungian Analyst

Introduction by
Sidney Handel

Contributing Authors
Esther De Vos
Thomas Kirsch
Dennis Merritt
June Singer
Marvin Spiegelman
Murray Stein

SIGO PRESS
BOSTON

 SIGO PRESS
25 New Chardon Street, #8748
Boston, Massachusetts 02214

Publisher and General Editor: Sisa Sternback
Associate Editor: Marc E. Romano

International Standard Book Number: 0-938434-28-4 (paperback)

Library of Congress Cataloging-in-Publication Data:
The Analytic Life.
    Consists of papers from a conference held in 1985.
    Includes bibliographies and index.
    1. Psychoanalysis — Congresses. I. De Vos, Esther.
[DNLM: 1. Psychoanalysis — congresses. WM 460 A5317 1985]
RC500.5.A53 1989 616.89″17″0922   88-18237

Printed in the USA

Table of Contents

The Analytic Life

Introduction

Sidney Handel, NESJA

It is the glory of God to conceal a thing; but the glory of kings is to search a matter out.
Proverbs 25:2

Twenty years ago there were fewer than three hundred practitioners of analytical psychology in the entire world. There are now more than that number in the United States alone, and nearly as many currently enrolled in American training programs. There are seven regional societies in the United States, each with its own training program, and the proliferation is not yet at an end.

C.G. Jung's contribution to twentieth-century thought has been enormous, and its full impact is yet to be fully realized. His ideas have influenced many disciplines, and it is not even clear that their principal effect will be in the area of psychotherapy itself. So naturally the Jungian "population explosion" is witnessed with considerable gratification by those committed to the analytic process.

Still, it cannot be denied that rapid growth has also entailed certain difficulties. For the ancients, the messengers of divinity would generally appear at a particular place. This was a way of saying that each location had its own tutelary spirit or, more prosaically, its own guiding principles. So it is with the various American societies and training programs. Each may be characterized by its own unique flavor. It is self-evident

ix

that this reality has its definite advantages. For one thing, people entering training now have some choice in determining what best serves their individual needs. Perhaps even more important is the idea that differences of attitude and emphasis, when contained within a common vessel, create tensions and dialectics which can serve to keep the spirit of analytical psychology creative and dynamic. This has been the case, many believe, on the international level.

However, as numbers and institutions grow and flourish along their somewhat separate lines, the difficulties of maintaining that common vessel grow apace. In the past, when most analysts knew one another at least by reputation, questions of mutual recognition and acceptance were determined, or left unsettled, on a very personal basis. The Jungian community functioned in many ways like an extended family. Relations between some "cousins" might have been problematic, but communication took place under the aegis of a form of kinship libido. But collateral branches of most families tend to go their independent ways, and kinship libido is not indefinitely extendible.

A few years ago, when the local societies were maturing, there developed in the United States a common desire to explore the nature of collegial relations in a more formal context. From this first emerged the irregular meetings of representatives of individual societies, and now the regular convocation of national conferences.

In 1985 it was the privilege of the New England Society of Jungian Analysts, one of the newer societies, to be the host of the meeting at the Parker House in Boston. The papers presented at the morning sessions of the 1985 National Conference of Jungian Analysts form the content of this publication.

The tendency in both national and international conferences has been twofold: papers are solicited on themes considered relevant to the principal theoretical and practical concerns of analytical psychology; at the same time, an attempt is made to focus some discussion on areas of tension and disagreement.

For the meeting in Boston, it was decided to try a somewhat different approach. An effort was made to bring colleagues together under the theme of what unites them rather than what divides them. To this end, papers were invited which dealt with areas that should be relevant to all analysts regardless of any conceptual differences. On one side this would include questions of how the Jungian approach is affected by the collective environment in which it exists. On the other, it would include certain existential factors which influence from within the practice of analysis and its meaning, as well as how the analyst himself is affected by his work.

It was intended, then, to explore "The Analytic Life" from both an extraverted and introverted perspective. In determining the choice of papers to be presented, the major emphasis was on the question of what the attendees, as "Jungians" and as analysts, share with each other.

Naturally the theme of unity must constellate its opposite. So it was particularly appropriate that the conference began with the most profound *separatio*.

In looking for papers which were of inclusive relevance, the Conference Committee was unable to accept any of the several proposals which dealt exclusively with issues pertaining to the concerns of the women members of the local societies.

The energy which flows around such concerns, however, is not to be denied. Upon being asked to do so, the Conference Committee was happy to provide its cooperation to several of the women involved in establishing a pre-conference meeting limited to attendance by women analysts and trainees.

The fantasy of masculine-feminine remains the structural metaphor for fundamental dichotomy. And so with proper enantiodromia, the analysts, whose work is so symbolic, began the conference of unity with a concrete separation of the sexes. For this pre-conference meeting, Jane Wheelwright was therefore invited by its organizers to present an address, and though that paper is not included in this collection, it was well received and spoke to the importance of maintaining differences that exist between the genders and yet honoring the important similarities that bind us as humans.

It may be said here that any gender issues and differences connect all analysts, male and female, to the general collective, and inevitably to each other. Gender issues are, however, but one set of forces which determine the manner in which analysts struggle to relate to the spirit of their times. Jung, for example, sought continuously to anchor his ideas in a scientific matrix. Yet his psychology is a symbolic one, and the symbol has two axes — the rational and the irrational. As a result, Jung's concepts have, as often as not, been of more appeal to those attracted to the "hidden" than to the verifiable realm of science. Indeed, much of the criticism of Jung's psychology, beginning even with Freud, was based on its "occultism."

The resulting tension between the mystical and scientific may actually be seen as a significant contribution of analytical psychology, since it pushes for a synthesis between the neoplatonic and Aristotelian viewpoints. This synthesis has remained philosophically and psychologically elusive, and the resulting tension provides the energy for a creative dialectic.

From the perspective of the individual analyst, the unresolved issues have contributed to forming a kind of collective identity crisis. Are analysts shamans, artists, and priests, or are they physicians, psychologists, and diagnosticians?

Each of the papers presented on the first official day of the conference dealt with facets of this identity question. Murray Stein discusses the changing ties to the psychological ground from which analytical psychology emerged; Dennis Merritt explains the relationship of that psychology to the world of science; and Esther De Vos suggests some parallels between analytical psychology and the occult world of Voodoo.

Questions of identity as reflected in ties to the collective environment in which the work takes place represent only one area in which analysts share a general interest. Another and perhaps more vital common concern has to do with what Jung called the "personal equation." The tools of the analytic trade include at one level only a space, two chairs, a clock, and facial tissues. These material factors fade in importance, of course, when contrasted with the true instruments of analysts, namely the psyches involved.

Even though all diploma analysts are presumed to have "successfully completed a satisfactory personal analysis" as a primary requirement of training, no practitioner can hold himself immune from the transformative effects of life's *via negativa* on their psyche. Old age, sickness, and consciousness of death continue the training of the analyst beyond the gaining of a diploma. And it would be exceedingly naive to assume that their effects must be always for the good.

Moreover, as ordinary human beings, analysts are enmeshed in a world of family, friends (and enemies), and neighbors. These bonds are affected by the work in many ways, conscious and unconscious. And, in turn, they affect the work in that same reciprocal fashion. What is brought to the consulting room and what is taken home from it mutually interpenetrate for better and for worse.

These factors shape the lenses through which life and the personality are seen. And they raise issues which transcend doctrinal disputes and differences of opinion and technique. They form the common elements of experience which are shared by necessity more than by choice.

No less escapable but more diffuse in its effects is the general question of suffering and analysis. It is a well-known temptation to imagine that one's own work or path is one of particular suffering, especially when that work is concerned with psyche or soul. Whether as a negative inflation or a misguided *imitatio*, this is especially seductive for analysts.

Yet there is some justification for this particular illusion. It is very often the case that people enter analysis to find relief from suffering. So to be an analyst is to be drawn again and again to the psyche's experience of its own suffering, and the analyst is forced to deal with his own suffering, if only to function adequately as a psychopomp.

Moreover, it can be asserted that many analysts were originally attracted to their profession through a fascination with their own psyches and their vicissitudes. Personal analysis generally begins well before training. So even if the suffering of the analyst is neither more nor less than everyone's, he is both pushed and pulled to try to relate more fully to it.

The effects of aging, of personal relationships and of the analyst's connection to suffering were the themes presented on the second day of the conference by June Singer, Thomas Kirsch, and J. Marvin Spiegelman.

Now a few words must be devoted to that which cannot be revealed. Parallel to the effort to find a commonality of theme was an attempt to achieve a more personal tone than is often attained at a formal meeting. For this reason the conference was given a format which differed from the usual. Rather than have the responses to the papers presented in the morning plenary sessions, they were reserved for another time and only a few brief comments and questions were accepted from the floor.

In the afternoon, simultaneous sessions were held at which the responses to the morning papers were presented. Under the guidance of moderators, extensive and intensive discussion was encouraged between the authors of the papers presented here, the respondents, and those attendees whose presence indicated a special interest in the particular topic.

This format was designed with a threefold intent. First, individuals had an opportunity to digest the morning's contents and to allow the psyche the time it so often needs to react. Introversion was served in this manner as well, since it is often the more extraverted personalities who are best able to respond quickly and publicly. Hence there was a possibility for individuals who participate more rarely to express their views and feelings.

It was hoped that this would be facilitated further in the context of smaller groups. This allowed for more intimacy and provided the opportunity for continuous dialogue, and even argument. Finally, individuals choosing which discussion group to join attended them with a now-informed interest in the topic, and this offered the promise of a more spirited participation.

Of course, each of these motivations provided its own shadow. For one thing, there was no way for individuals to attend all the afternoon discussion groups. Since constraints of time, space, and resources have forced the decision not to publish the afternoon events, what transpired there must remain hidden to many attendees at the conference as well as to the general public.

The matter of things left unrevealed, however, is also a result of the goal of the proceedings. As life itself may be imagined as a masked ball, so the particular personae are more or less appropriate to the individual event. The small group allows for a more personal revelation of the personality. Even when there is no particular taboo against the excessive disclosure of the personal life of the analyst, a proper modesty limits the publication of what is shown, as well as the making of that display possible.

In keeping with the innovative aspect of the discussion format, the results were uneven. It is, however, satisfying to report that where things went well, they went very well indeed. One measure of this was the degree to which facets of the psyche which would still be concealed under the cloak of words were able to emerge for those present. At such moments the goal of the conference was achieved.

Paradoxically, then, the essence of the meeting lay in that which must remain unpublished. It is with this thought that thanks are to be extended to the respondents. They are William Bulay, Philip Zabriskie, Mary Loomis, Jane Wheelwright, James Hall, and Sally Parks.

They and the main speakers are due an extra portion of gratitude, especially because of a (naively) unexpected consequence of the format.

The two hour give-and-take sessions called for a far more than customary expenditure of energy on the part of all active participants. Sincere thanks are a far from adequate recompense for the generosity of spirit that was called for and repeatedly provided.

Gratitude must also be expressed to the moderators of the afternoon sessions. Drawn from the membership of the New England Society of Jungian Analysts, they are Ira Sharkey, Elizabeth Stevenson, David Lindorff, Russell Holmes, Joel Covitz, and Robert Bosnak. Their efforts were key and also far greater than might have been reasonable to expect.

Fortunately, transformations of conscious attitudes are more properly attainable than alterations of ancient spiritual poetry. So if the afternoon sessions must remain concealed, Proverbs may be paraphrased to say that it was the pleasure of Kings and Queens to search the matter out. The conference was inaugurated by the separation of men and women. It reached the end of its celebration with a real masked ball appropriate to the Halloween weekend of its schedule. On the dance floor, to the sound of music both Orphic and Hermetic, there was a joyous reunification of the opposites.

How to generate kinship libido is not adequately known. It is clear, however, that personal connection is one matrix out of which it may emerge. It is the hope of the New England Society that the conference, in its entirety, may have helped form such a matrix.

In keeping with the spirit of C.G. Jung, his followers aim not for perfection but for wholeness. And to be whole every process must include its own anticlimax. So it must be said that the ball was followed by the last event of the conference—the business meeting. Here it was, of course, impossible to ignore some of the problems of the present and the intimations of the future. But even to those present, these remain partially veiled and in readiness for future convocations.

Finally, thanks are due to the fellow members of the Conference Committee, to Soren Ekstrom and John Haule, for their creation of the 1985 meeting. They are free of any blame which might accrue from the remarks in this introduction.

Sidney Handel
Boston, 1986

1

Solutio and *Coagulatio* in Analytical Psychology

One Man's View of Where our Field is Today

Murray Stein

These comments on the state of analytical psychology and Jungian analysis today are partly a subjective confession and partly, I believe, fairly accurate observations of what is going on with others in the field as well. It has seemed to me for some years now that our field needs to dissolve and go through a "midlife crisis" by breaking up old structures and commitments and reforming around a new cluster of central ideas and methods. This is reflective of my own chronological position in life, and so my sensitivity to this need may be colored by a personal need to embark upon such a psychological transformation myself. But I will take the risk here of speaking my mind anyway, in the hope of provoking a discussion at least.

It has seemed to me that the classical consensus in Jungian psychology has lost its life force and that an era of breakup (*solutio*) has set in. Personifying our field, it is experiencing a loss of identity in this era of change, and questioning its own value and integrity. Shadow contents are pressing forward to be taken notice of and integrated. The unconscious contents that are emerging as the persona breaks down seem to cluster around the oldest repression in our field, psychoanalysis and

1

Freud. I believe that a reevaluation of the Jung-Freud dispute is going on, that the preeminent position of Jung is being relativized, and that Freud is being taken up for reexamination. Especially the new developments that have been occurring in our collective unconsciousness during the last three decades — the changes that have taken place in psychoanalysis as a result of the impact of English object relations theory, of Kohut's work in this country, and of the other modern psychoanalysts whose works were cited by the speakers in last year's national conference (Klaif, Satinover, Ulanov, Machtiger, and Ekstrom) — are being taken up and becoming gradually assimilated in our new collective identity. We are today, in my view, in the midst of a collective transformation process, and this will eventuate, over the next ten years or so, a new identity for the practitioner of analytical psychology. What this "new person" will be called — a "Jungian analyst," an "analytical psychologist" or something else — is unclear at this point. What is quite clear is that our field is going through a profound transformation from what one could call the "classical consensus" of Jungian thought and philosophy to something that will integrate the repressed elements of psychoanalysis.

I believe, further, that the radical voice of James Hillman in our field was an augur of this transformation, coming some ten years ahead of time and clearly calling for a fundamental transformation in the way we see, think, and work. I don't believe, however, that the field will take the road he created, but rather that his influence will turn out to have helped create the climate in which the changes now taking place were made possible. Hillman questioned fundamental assumptions and identifications, and this broke the ground of the field's identity formations and prepared the way for transformation.

This is my general confession and my thesis. Let me now spell out the parts of it a bit further.

The Breakup of the Classical Consensus

Andrew Samuels' recent book, *Jung and the Post-Jungians*, identifies the major school in the field of analytical psychology as the "classical school." In this school he lists thirty-eight analyst/authors, which in his estimate would make up forty-eight percent of the field. That is today. If we go back ten or fifteen years, the figure would certainly have been higher, perhaps in the seventy-five to eighty-five percent range. What have cut into the hegemony of the classical school, according to Samuels, are two other competing schools, the developmental (London) and the archetypal (Hillman). Of these, the archetypal is the newer and the smaller. The developmental school, according to Samuels, would today make up thirty-five percent of the field. The remaining seventeen percent belongs to the archetypal school. One can quibble with Samuels about numbers and about the relative strength of the various schools, even about the terms he uses to describe their differences, but one thing is clear: a field that was largely "classical" is rather rapidly breaking up into schools of often extremely different viewpoints.

It is equally clear to me that most individual analysts in our field today carry the tensions of each of these schools within themselves. There are relatively few analysts who practice in a "pure" way in any one of these three schools. All of us have been influenced, I imagine, to at least a small degree, by the schools to which we do *not* subscribe.

The archetypalist challenge came from within the field itself, as an extension of some of Jung's thoughts and the refutation or repression of others. The concept of the Self was relativized, the symbol was deconstructed, images were given centrality, compensation was disregarded, the theory of opposites was taken metaphorically, and imagination was given the highest position. This school has appealed most powerfully to persons who were trained in the classical Zürich mode, least powerfully to those who were trained in developmentalist climates.

The developmentalist school of London, originated by Fordham, has drawn its chief heresies from psychoanalysis, especially from the trends of psychoanalysis that developed in England under the leadership of Melanie Klein and Anna Freud and then branched into the schools spawned by Winnicott, Fairbairn, Guntrip, Bion, Mahler, Spitz and others. Where the developmental school has challenged the classical consensus is on the importance of childhood (especially infancy), the need for analysis of personal history and development, and the detailed analysis of transference and countertransference. These were the major weak spots in the classical consensus as it developed under Jung's own interests and biases in Zürich. Fordham has been at least as controversial in our field as Hillman, and I believe the contents he introduced into the body of our discipline will have the more far-reaching, transformative influence.

Lifting the Repression on Psychoanalysis

When Jung and Freud parted ways, Freud announced that he was withdrawing his libido from Jung; and Jung, as Satinover has demonstrated (*Chiron* 1985), repressed Freud. Each would continue to be influenced by the other, but that influence would be hidden from view and perhaps even from the consciousness of each. Jung's repression of psychoanalysis led to his distortions of what psychoanalysis was, and to distortions about how his own analysis was different. As the history of the field is being reconstructed, it is becoming clearer that their differences were not always what they said they were and that each was entwined with the other in many subtle, unsuspected ways. I believe, too, that Freud's intellectual influence on Jung has been sometimes overemphasized.

In the classical consensus, an unofficial taboo was placed upon Freud and his writings and even upon the writings of his followers. And so it began to seem that analytical psychology was a depth psychological tradition wholly unto itself. In its literature there was little reference to authors or works outside of the inner circle. Epigones would quote Jung, and Jung would occasionally refer to some of them. The tradition began to isolate itself and soon became rich enough internally to support a kind of autonomous culture. Methods of treatment, clinical theories, metapsychological viewpoints, cultural commentaries, case reports, interpretations of religion, culture, and myth all wove together to create a body of literature with little or no reference to the wider field of psychoanalysis. The only time reference would be made to Freud or to psychoanalytic thinkers would be to use them as contrast points or to rebut their shortsightedness. In the classical texts of our tradition — Jung's own writings after 1913, Baynes, Neumann, Jacobi, Harding, von Franz, Emma Jung, Toni Wolff, and such Americans as James Kirsch, Edinger, Henderson, Whitmont — there is little sense that the authors are students of Freudian or modern psychoanalysis in any disciplined sense, although there *are* occasional references to Freud and to psychoanalytic writings. But more and more one had the sense of an autonomous Jungian tradition, which learned from history of religions, from anthropology, from classical studies, from philosophy and literature, but *not* from other clinical schools, psychoanalytic or other. This gave a sort of non-clinical flavor to the literature and turned it into something akin to cultural hermeneutics. Until recently, there were three Jungian journals in this country, all of them focused on non-clinical, cultural issues. Until *Chiron*, the only clinical journal in English was the developmentalist *Journal of Analytical Psychology*. But this was the nature of the classical consensus, because it followed Jung's own later non-clinical interests in culture and religion.

In the last ten years, however, the field has begun to change radically, and Freud and psychoanalysis are no longer the taboo contents they once were. As this material has come flooding into our field during these last years, the shadow has come along, creating anxiety about identity, integrity, and self-worth.

There may have been a period in the heyday of the classical consensus when Jungians felt they had the world by the tail. They understood the psyche; they knew how therapy worked and how it healed; they had the methods necessary for the treatment of individual and collective ills; and if only the world would listen, it would only be a matter of time until things were resolved. The other clinical schools were looked upon as hopelessly benighted and bogged down in superficial concerns of adjustment, symptom relief, or obsessive analysis of the personal unconscious. I do not believe Jungians would generally speak this way today, at least not with much self-assurance. Once the main structural edifice of the classical consensus began to weaken and tilt, the repressed shadow of old and new psychoanalytic thought began to rush in and to create anxiety and insecurity, and one result of this development was to go back to our history. The appearance of the repressed shadow of classical Jungianism made it much more difficult than before to deny history and development.

In the classical consensus, a view of history had been created that saw our father-hero (Jung) outgrowing his mentor (Freud) and going deeper and further in his pioneering explorations than the more timid ancestor had gone. Jung's thought outstripped Freud's, granted that he had the advantage of standing on the shoulders of a giant. What Jung had done was to risk all for the sake of further and deeper psychological, scientific explorations, and what he had discovered rendered Freud's discoveries limited and obsolete. What was not seen in this version of history was Jung's repression of Freud and the consequent distortions. Jung led the field away from developmental issues, transference and countertransference, childhood and infancy, and personal psychodynamics. These issues were taken up in Jung's thought, but symbolically, and they thus became relativized by the plethora of archetypal themes Jung discovered in the unconscious. They were disposed of by saying they were too limiting in scope to allow for genuine psychological growth and individuation. What needed to be done, according to the classical consensus, was to go on discovering still more archetypal symbols, more amplifications of patients' dreams from world religions and fairy tales, and more evidence of archetypal structures from neurology, biology, anthropology, and ethnology. There was no point in investigating infancy, childhood, transference, treatment outcomes, unresolved problems in psychological functioning, etc. These kinds of questions were left to the shadow field, psychoanalysis, which did meanwhile continue developing its own clinical and theoretical tradition precisely along these lines.

As Charles Klaif detailed in his excellent paper at last year's national conference, the field of psychoanalysis has gone through several epochal transformations from drive theory to ego theory to self theory. It has reached a point where a convergence with Jungian though has become feasible. But in order for Jungians to benefit from this possible rapprochement, we will have to learn what led the psychoanalysts to this point, and this is very much akin to discovering the secret life of the shadow. There is something forbidden and taboo about it, and this kind of secret knowledge stirs up deep anxieties and questions of adequacy. There is a point in the process of transformation where the life of the shadow looks superior to the life of consciousness; it seems to have more energy and intelligence; new life lies precisely in what had been earlier discarded and neglected. And this is the way modern psychoanalysis appears to many of us Jungians today. We can safely pronounce this to be a compensatory distortion.

In opening up the path into this region of shadow, the image of Jung, our hero and father, has become altered. Quoting from Jung to prove a point is no longer fashionable in Jungian circles, although I must admit it is still done. But the more "advanced" colleagues wince when it happens. It is embarrassing, because the figure of Jung no longer carries the aura of numinosity. Jung is no longer a symbolic Self figure in the field of analytical psychology. This is a loss and a gain. Certainly he is still an orienting figure, and his works are still the basic texts, but in the present state of *solutio* Jung is no longer the only orienting figure. Monotheism has given way, I hope not to polytheism, though this may indeed be the case. Now instead of quoting only Jung for authority, one quotes Jung and. . . Winnicott, Kohut, Jacobson, Klein, and even Freud. But at least there is now a collection of seminal figures, and among these is Jung, perhaps as *primus inter pares* but certainly surrounded by a group of not-too-long-ago totally unfamiliar names.

The Appearance of the Anima

The current state of *solutio* in the field of analytical psychology is the result, I believe, of a natural aging process. This kind of change is inherent within traditions. It is a stage along the way toward growing up and growing older. Not only is this a time when the elements of depth psychology that Jung repressed are advancing to the fore, as evidenced by the rather remarkable interest Jungians are taking in old and new psychoanalytic thought, but it is also a time when a psychology of the anima has appeared from within our own womb. I am referring to archetypal psychology.

Archetypal psychology is, according to Samuels (and I agree with him), a significant minority position within the field of analytical psychology. As a distinct, separate school within the confines of our field, it will not, I believe, become much stronger than it presently is, largely because it has all too obvious deficits as a theory and praxis. It is, however, an important critical stance over against the classical position. Archetypal psychology speaks for the lost soul of analytical psychology. It supports the spirit of the *puer*, the romance of the anima, the soulful, willful young rebel's hatred of history, of structure, or regimentation, of institutionalization. It is a Hermetic stance within the monolithic heaviness of classical Jungianism, slipping into the crevices and through the keyholes, peeping and spying, telling tales, flaunting psychic images, attacking truisms and dogmas. Its adolescent spirit has made it intolerable to many of our aging colleagues of the classical and developmentalist persuasions. Archetypal psychology's glaring deficiencies have been pointed out and lambasted in many journal articles, and as a separate clinical or theoretical standpoint it is perhaps untenable, a wayward orphan. Yet it is a call to the anima, to depth, to the detail in psyche's wonderland, to images of color and texture, to an eros of the inner life and of imagination. It is a call back to youth, even to childhood and infancy. Its audacity is perhaps made possible by its confidence that the center will hold.

Coagulatio, the New Integration

It is doubtless too soon to speak of what a new synthesis will bring after this turmoil and the dissolution of old structures is past. We are still far too much in the midst of *solutio* to be able to say what the outcome will look like. What will our identity be after this crisis is over? Will we all become crypto- or pseudo-neo-Freudians? Will we lose identity altogether and never get it back? Or will we become reborn classical Jungians and leave off hankering after these tempting new byways? Or will we become some mongrelized syncretism? Who knows? One thing is certain: it is still too early to attempt a synthesis. When one does come about, it will doubtless be a surprise, a product of the unconscious and not of our deliberate devising.

Samuels attempts to begin tying together some strands in his *Jung and the Post-Jungians*, and he makes interesting connections between the archetypal and developmental schools, trying, as it were, to tie together the two extreme frayed ends of our discipline. I believe this is premature, although it is not without its interest and possible value for some individuals. My own feeling is that the stew needs to cook more, that *solutio* needs to become thicker and more chaotic before it solidifies into a new form. The classical consensus is still far too strong to permit a genuine transformation. This transformation will begin at the edges, I believe, and eventually the paradigm will shift when about twenty percent of the field has gone through the process individually. That point may be still a decade away. I am a poor prophet, however, and would not place much money on my estimates.

In the meantime, what is to be done?

Last spring five of us, two women and three men, Jungians, spent a hilarious afternoon in a car between Giverney and Paris. The psyche was activated by the day, the place, the combination of personalities, and for two or three hours we played a game of fantasy. The theme of the fantasy was "Bouffing and being bouffed." *Bouffer* is French slang for eating crudely. In the hilarity, it seemed that the wisest course was to allow ourselves to be bouffed, not to resist, and that only through the process of being bouffed, of surrendering to the powers that were seeking to bouff us, could genuine transformation come about. It was a good and positive thing to become bouffed, to enter the belly of the bouffeur, and to suffer the process of being digested.

In reading the excellent papers from last year's conference, published in *Quadrant* this past spring, I noticed a recurrent theme, spoken of in the language of Piaget: "assimilation and accommodation." This is a polite way of saying "bouffing and being bouffed." So far I believe our field has been bouffing, by assimilating influences, and this has produced a great loosening of the grip of the classical Jungian consensus. But the center has held, and our identity has not radically changed. We have become Jungians who know a lot more about Freud and later psychoanalytic thinking and the archetypalists. But transformation has not taken place, identity has not shifted, clinical practice has been altered in minor ways but not in major ones. The next stage will be more profound, I believe. We will be bouffed: accommodation, not assimilation, will take place. We will disappear, and this process will affect our field to the core and will leave nothing unchanged. A new field will be born from the ashes of the old, and its name will be. . . who knows?

2

Jungian Psychology and Science

A Strained Relationship

Dennis Merritt

Our topic at this conference is the analytic life, one aspect of which is how we as analysts see ourselves in relation to our collective milieu. One very important collective to which we are related is the scientific community. Our relationship to it is of personal importance to me, since I made a sudden switch from science to Jungian psychology, going from a Ph.D. in insect pathology at Berkeley to the Jung Institute in Zürich. The shift left a decisive split in my psyche, a split with which I continue to struggle. It has sensitized me to the problems which arise between Jungians and the scientific community, and it has forced me to look both critically and sympathetically at each side in an attempt to heal the split. Scientists and analysts stand to benefit from such an attempt to better understand and respect each other.

As a Jungian analyst, I will approach the topic as most analysts would, by calling upon my personal dream biography. These biographies grow over the years in our dream books and journals, accompanying our outer journey and setting the stage for major shifts in our lives. Our inner psychic life becomes as real as, if not more real than, "outer" reality. Experience shows us that our fantasies, images, and powerful dreams

11

underlie and shape our outer experiences in profound ways. Although this inner life is hidden from others, by individually becoming conscious of it and fixing it in writing, painting, or just in memory, we double our life experience and total biography. Sharing "big" dreams with those Jungians closest to us provides a depth of intimacy, understanding, and connection unique to our profession.

It was through my dreams that I discovered that my scientific sensitivities were somehow suffering at the hands of my Jungian training. When I realized that other scientists were experiencing similar difficulties, I began to question what lay behind the strained relationship between Jungian psychology and science. The dream series which follows illustrates my evolution from science to Jungian psychology, as well as some of the problems generated by the transition.

I had the following dream while I was working on my dissertation on insect pathology and simultaneously developing an avid interest in Jung.

> I'm looking at the crumbling, burned-out inside of a building with my wife. It may be our place, or somehow connected with us.
> Now I'm at the beginning of a street named after a countercultural friend who lives at the end of the street. It's below the house mentioned above. To my left is a beautiful modern two-story house with a party going on. I'm inside now, walking toward a table where James Hillman and Jacob Bronowski are talking to each other. I'm going to be introduced to them.

At the time, I saw Hillman as an innovative and scholarly Jungian thinker and writer, and Bronowski, who impressed me with his "The Ascent of Man" series on PBS, as a noted scientist with a humanistic background.

This dream pointed my life in a new direction. It turned me towards a synthesis of Jung and science in which a more open, innovative, and questioning attitude among Jungians might embrace a humanistic, scientific attitude. In this paper I will attempt to develop this idea.

The shift away from my solid scientific standpoint was depicted in a dream I had after being accepted at the Jung Institute in Zürich, and while I was still writing my thesis on a nuclear polyhedrosis virus of the beet armyworm.

> I wander away from an entomology picnic with my advisor, an

archetypal German entomologist friend, and some other entomologists. I go into the adjoining woods and crawl into a large stump with an oval-shaped cavity lined with a thick, green, moss-like material. The entomologists come looking for me but they don't discover my location.

At that point my path was leading me away from entomology. I was being protected and nourished by the unconscious while a new direction developed.

Off I went to Zürich, and soon became immersed in analysis and the training program. Two and a half years later, I had a dream which strongly indicated to me that something was amiss in my scientific background.

Beneath the softball field of the one-room country school that I attended in rural Wisconsin was a huge cavern filled with white rabbits. As one end of the cavern was my archetypal Berkeley entomologist friend working with some test tubes.

The dream seemed to be saying that there was an enormous amount of unconscious scientific creativity in my psyche. At that time I was reconnecting with my scientific side, teaching high-school biology to support my training at the Jung Institute. I had also begun to consider my thesis topic, which I hoped would provide an opportunity to combine my Jungian and scientific interests. Eventually a thesis emerged, entitled "Synchronicity Experiments with the *I Ching* and their Relevance to the Theory of Evolution."[1] The work began with an overwhelming insight I had while waiting at a Zürich train station. This revelation was followed by a flood of ideas and several "big" dreams hinting at the archetypal basis of my work.

One of the last dreams I had in Zürich along these lines was the following:

An older scientist is doing research on otter dogs. He has asked me to assist him on the project. I don't know if I will have the time.

Here I was being asked by a scientist to do scientific work on a project involving a creature which is a combination of a wild water animal (otter) and a domestic land animal (dog)—a synthesis of opposites. But was I ready to devote my psychic energy to it?

These dreams made me question what was happening to my scientific side while I was undergoing Jungian training. In Zürich, there was such a strong emphasis on the irrational, the intuitive, and the inner life that I began to feel a little off-balance. It also became clear that the scientific attitude was somehow despised and discredited there. At a Jungian gathering, a good scientific friend of mine told me that he felt the analysts present were condescending toward his scientific attitude and that they seemed to think their viewpoint was superior. Another scientist, who was in the training program with me, also mentioned several disparaging remarks about scientists he had heard in Zürich. One person said a relative was neurotic because he was a mathematician, that he had fled from his feelings into mathematics. Another colleague described students at the Zürich Technical University as mostly obsessive types, loving order and control. Students in control seminars remarked that their analysands should get out of science and take up more human and irrational pursuits in order to align their personalities. The collective picture of a scientist was that of a cold, rational, dull, and unfeeling person interested in lifeless things.

Science itself and the products of the technological revolution have come under even harsher attack. Von Franz referred to the technological exploration of nature as devilish and destructive, "extraverted restlessness which goes on and on beyond natural measure."[2] A Time Magazine article described such inventors as Whitney, Edison, and the Wright brothers as "tinkerers with tunnel vision," and observed that Americans are growing wary of innovation.[3] Jung had seen as dangerous the scientist's tendency to view science as an end in itself, exclusive of feeling, fantasy, and vision. Jung saw this leading not only to the

> high differentiation and specialization of the particular functions concerned, but also to their detachment from the world and from life, as well as to a multiplication of specialized fields which gradually lose all connection with one another. The result is an impoverishment and dessication not merely in the specialized fields but in the psyche of every man who has differentiated himself up and sunk down to the specialist level.[4]

J. Gary Sparks, in a Zürich thesis entitled "The Wounded Finger: Anchorage for Soul and Sense in Technology," warns against adopting a stereotypic view of science and scientists.[5] He points out how the analyst with such a viewpoint is in danger of violating something in the personality of his scientist analysand, thinking of healing in terms of getting the analysand "out of science." A better approach might be for the analyst to develop an understanding of scientific creativity and then to see his task as that of deepening the scientific spirit in the analysand. For a narrow-minded scientist, salvation may lie in discovering the essence of his or her craft, and not in abandoning it. But to help a scientist overcome his or her difficulties, we, as analysts, must move beyond our own myopia.

Although the excesses of science are fairly obvious, we must not throw out the baby with the bath water. Science is a powerful amalgam of creative fantasy, method, discipline, and attention to detail which has enabled us to look deeply into the structure and order of the universe, as well as to consciously manipulate the universe to our own ends, be they constructive or destructive. We have stolen fire from the gods and unless we learn how to use that fire wisely, we will destroy all of life, whether by nuclear fire, pollution, overpopulation, or whatever. We cannot give the fire back to the gods; we cannot forsake our consciousness. It will take a more humane use of science — not an abandonment of it — to help us out of our predicament.

For a balanced perspective, an analyst should have an appreciation of the scientific method and the rigor of its approach. The degree of honesty and discipline necessary to extract the secrets of nature is no less demanding than that required to discover truths about ourselves and our psychic operations. An analyst's pejorative attitude towards science may also affect the analytical process. Although many scientists are only glorified technicians, science itself depends upon the creative acts of its most brilliant contributors. Scientific creativity is not distinct from other forms of creativity. The danger of mishandling a creative process is just as acute with a scientist as it is with any other artist.

The scientist himself should be helped to realize that creative insights, and new directions and perspectives, come not from conscious effort alone but largely from "hunches" and "ah-ha" experiences which have their source in the irrational. The disciplined, directed, conscious efforts of the mind to focus on a problem take the scientist only so far. After that he hits a wall, draws a blank, gets stuck. No amount of will or energy can force an insight or solution. It is then that the scientist, or any other artist, must turn the process over to the unconscious. At this time he or she may have dreams about a wounded finger, which, since the fingers are symbolic of creativity, indicates a overly conscious approach to the creative process. A *yin*, receptive, "waiting upon" attitude is necessary. The creative scientist must recognize the importance of this phase and develop work habits and attitudes to accommodate it. The realm of the irrational has its own rhythm, and the creative scientist must learn to adjust to it.[6]

The depression, anxiety, and uncertainty that beset a creative scientist when no insight or solution comes is not unlike that of the "blocked" poet or writer. The scientist may even experience a small existential crisis in which he calls into question the meaning of his work. It is vitally important that the analyst not try to analyze the depression away, but rather try to understand its relationship to the creative process. The rhythm of the unconscious cannot be ignored, forced, or damaged. It is incumbent upon the analyst to be aware of this rhythm in creative analysands, including creative scientists.

The unconscious also has its own order and ordering capacity which extends, via synchronicity, into the broader environment. How many great discoveries have been flukes or accidents?[7] The rational, scientific mind can be profoundly affected by learning to appreciate this broader aspect of the creative process.

The creative scientist is not without feeling or fantasy. Intense passion often drives and sustains him through many dead ends and the tedious, repetitive work of verification. The results — in the cold logic and neat formulas appearing in scientific publications — give no clue to the intensity of life energy that sustains him. Without a playful and completely free fantasy, the scientist could never come to imagine a new way of putting things together or perceiving "reality." The psychological root of the scientific process could be seen as an eros relationship between scientists and the material realm.

Von Franz states that a scientist partly channels eros into his profession and to the ideas he loves.[8] Hillman sees the rise of science as due to the projection of the anima into matter.[9] Alchemy preceded modern science — as a compensation for the ethereal, spiritual other-worldliness of Christianity — by working with matter and projecting unconscious contents onto matter and material dynamics. Even today, our most advanced science, nuclear physics, can use terms like "charm," "flavor," "truth" and "beauty" in naming the qualities of the states of sub-atomic particles.

Analysts should realize the potential for a symbolic interpretation of a scientific creation, invention, or discovery. Just as the product of a painter's endeavor can be analyzed to further his individuation process, so too a scientific work can be psychologically analyzed. Dream work can help put a scientist in harmony with the phases of his creative work as well as suggest to him specific projects on which to work. Dream work can reshape the content of the scientific endeavor. For a more thorough treatment of this and other aspects of scientific creativity on the archetypal level (as well as sample dreams), I refer the reader to Sparks' diploma thesis mentioned above. Most of the preceding material on creativity has come from this thesis. Let me close this section by quoting Sparks' perception of the relationship between individuation and scientific creativity.

> [A] value of scientific research in the context of individuation is that it constantly knocks "the illusion of the supremacy of consciousness"[10] out of the researcher. The scientist is often in a situation where he or she is "absolutely in need of a creative solution,"[11] the precondition for experiencing the greater power of the personality. This presupposes that the scientist begins to distinguish between the ego's and the larger personality's thoughts, between the power of one's control and those that are not. As individuation could be called that movement towards acknowledging and listening to something in one which is bigger than oneself, of gradually realizing that one is simply more than "I," situations which bring one to the end of one's wits, and which call forth the powers of "not I," necessarily foster this development.[12]

I would now like to turn my attention to an area of Jungian theory which causes the scientific community much consternation. This concerns the peculiar way in which Jung talked about archetypes as the residue of past experiences, repeated over and over again.

> From the scientific, causal standpoint the primitive image can be conceived as a mnemic deposit, an imprint or engram (Semon) which has arisen through condensation of countless processes of a similar kind. In this respect it is a precipitate, and therefore a typical basic form, of certain ever recurring psychic experiences.[13]
>
> It seems to me that their [archetypes] origin can only be explained by assuming them to be deposits of the constantly repeated experiences of humanity. We may assume that the archetypes are recurrent impressions made by subjective reactions. Archetypes apparently are impressions of ever repeated typical experiences.[14]

This manner of describing the origin of archetypes is disturbing to a scientific mind. Nothing currently accepted in evolutionary theory can begin to conceive of inheritance in terms of "precipitates" and "deposits." The use of such terms sounds prescientific and archaic, and leads one to question Jung's thinking and scientific grounding. Unfortunately these terms remind a biologist of Lamarckism, a theory of evolution predating Darwin, and anathema to the scientific community. Larmarck proposed that organisms could pass on traits acquired during their lifetimes. (Giraffes, for example, obtained their long necks by stretching their necks. The longer neck, acquired during a lifetime, was then passed on to the offspring). This hypothesis has never received any scientific proof and is in great disrepute in the scientific community.

In the "nature versus nurture" controversy, the nurture argument has long been in vogue, especially in American scientific thinking. The behaviorists have maintained a virtual stranglehold on universities, while Freudians with their *tabula rasa* view of the newborn's mind have dominated the depth psychological perspective in clinical psychology. Human behavior is seen by the behaviorists to be the result of social and environmental conditioning. Jung's archetypal hypothesis clearly falls on the nature/inheritance end of the spectrum, and is therefore well outside mainstream theory. However, the tide is beginning to turn with the rise of sociobiology and ethology, the recognition of the work of Konrad Lorenz, and the discovery of innate releasing mechanisms. We can begin to see a place for Jung's archetypal hypothesis within neo-Darwinian theory now that genetic traits have been recognized as the basis for behavior in animals, and perhaps even in us. Behavioral traits that have evolutionary value survive and are passed on to offspring through genes. The inheritance of particularly human patterns of emotion, perception, response, and development, as well as the tendency to produce typical psychic images, may fall within the parameters of a developing modern theory.

Jung's focus and forte was his recognition of recurrent themes and patterns in the interior life of humanity — in dreams, fantasies, images, etc. Other disciplines have failed to appreciate Jung's theory because of the complexity of his thought, his strongly introverted orientation, his emphasis on the irrational and intuitive, his dependence on personal experience for an understanding of the psyche, and the jargon which evolved after his death. As Jungians, we in turn have often failed to see how our theory is related to discoveries in other fields.

Enter Anthony Stevens. His book, *Archetypes*,[15] "put it all together," so to speak, berating Jungians for staying in their own little world. Stevens attempted to put archetypal theory on a sound biological basis by linking it to concepts in diverse areas. His writings led the noted anthropologist Victor Turner to apply the archetypal hypothesis to rituals and stages of life.

In a paper delivered in New England in 1984, entitled "Thoughts on the Psychobiology of Religion and the Neurobiology of Archetypal Experience,"[16] Stevens presented a cogent summary of his view of archetypes and raised some important issues. He spoke of archetypes as innate neuropsychic centers able to initiate, control, and mediate the behavioral characteristics common to *all* human beings. Every person, he proposed, is born with an archetypal base that presupposes the natural human life cycle. Stevens linked his theory to Piaget's concept that mental development proceeds through a series of innate stages, to Fox's idea that every individual has an inherited program for learning, and to Harlow's suggestion that social development relies on the maturation of a sequence of affectional systems. Stevens sees humans as having a psychophysical system with an inherited structure, function, and life cycle. As individuals go through life, the system accepts and absorbs the individual's life history. Each of us experiences only the personal aspect of our development, and remains in large part unaware of the phylogenetic blueprint from which it proceeds. Thus it becomes easy to see why analysts often adopt the viewpoint of behaviorists and learning theorists, who ascribe human behavior entirely to the conditioning each individual undergoes during his lifetime.

The archetypal hypothesis, Stevens finds, is being discovered and expounded in a variety of disciplines. Gestalt psychology has Kohler's isomorphs; developmental psychology has Bowlby's behavioral systems; the biologist Mayr speaks of open programs; Konrad Lorenz of innate releasing mechanisms; the anthropologist Fox of a biogrammer; and the psycholinguist Chomsky of a language acquisition device. These various approaches to archetypal processes may eventually find unity in the field of neurobiology. Stevens sees the beginning of such a synthesis in the possibility of neurological loci for archetypal functions (Henry and Stephens, 1977;[17] Maclean,[18] Stevens, 1982[19]) and in the neurological role dreams may play in integrating ontogenetic and phylogenetic aspects of the psyche (Jouvet, 1975[20], Smith *et al.*, 1974[21] Winson, 1978[22]). The

archetypal hypothesis may well prove to be the principle capable of unit-
ing all the natural sciences and establishing a unified science of humanity.[23]

Stevens relates neurobiology to Jungian concepts and foresees possible dangers to the psyche in the developing area of neurobiology. He
uses terms such as "left hemispheric imperialism" to relate neurobiology to Jung's perception that materialism in Western culture coincided
with the overdevelopment of the extraverted thinking function and the
repression of introverted feeling and intuition. The left cerebral hemisphere of the brain is more involved with analytical, sequential, logical
processes, while the right hemisphere functions intuitively, recognizes
patterns and is more holistic. Stevens warns that if we come to think
of psychic functions in terms of neuro-anatomy and neurochemistry, we
may too easily downgrade our impressions of what it is like to live these
neurobiological events. We are in danger of losing the poetry and dignity of our minds. The primacy of the psyche is paramount, with neurobiology *serving* it, not usurping it.[24]

One cannot help but become infected by the enthusiasm of Stevens'
writings and by his brilliant synthesis. *Archetypes*, however, has an unsettling undercurrent which, upon closer examination, explains the sus-
picion and fear with which Jung's archetypal hypothesis has been viewed.
It also illustrates a fundamental misuse of science, namely the backing
up of a particular viewpoint by drawing upon the solid sense one gets
from hard-won data and the use of rigorous experimental methods. Selec-
tively choosing which experiments and data to include, while ignoring
those which are contradictory or ambiguous, also gives a misleading level
of scientific support to Stevens' biased viewpoint.

An excellent critique is offered by Claire Douglas in her review of
Archetypes, entitled "Biology and Archetypal Theory," which appeared
in the *San Francisco Jung Institute Library Journal*.[25] What is disturbing about the archetypal hypothesis is that it proposes that there is something built-in and unchangeable in human nature. Stevens presents
archetypes as biological and fraught with pathological consequences aris-
ing from moving too far from the basic patterns. He draws upon genetics, hormones, neurophysiology, and behavior to make the following
statement:

A careful sifting of available evidence makes it clear that sexual differentiation is not nearly as malleable or culturally relative as contemporary prejudices would have us believe. It seems probable that significant differences between political, social and economic roles of men and women are determined by genetics. Contemporary confusions over gender roles, and the sexual aberration and social insecurity to which these confusions give rise, provide a vivid illustration of the misery that can be caused when biological reality is perverted in the cause of political dogma.[26]

Stevens uses secondary rather than primary sources to support his idea of the inevitability of male dominance. He concludes that

> Though it is indisputable that women have, until recently, endured low status in our society and have been subject to masculine exploitation, it is hard to avoid the conclusion that men are better equipped by nature to excel in a vast range of political, cultural and physical activities. There are and always have been women of outstanding ability, but even the brightest of them seem to lack those para-intellectual qualities which determine success in creative work, namely perseverance, aggression and ambition — all of which are known to be enhanced by the presence of testosterone in the blood stream and are probably due to differences in cerebral development as well.[27]

Douglas also warns that Stevens' definition of the archetypally human culture as warring, supremacist, and aristocratic could be used to justify fascism. Stevens says this about war and the need for enemies:

> A society surrounded by enemies is unified and strong, a society without enemies divided and lax. Men in groups are the same the whole world over: when there are no outsiders to fight, they turn on their compatriots. For a rush of adrenaline and a cure for boredom, for camaraderie and thrills, there is nothing like a good scrap.[28]

His view of the male archetype and the archetypal society seems to make war nearly inevitable:

> The unpalatable fact is that the propensity which men show in the first half of life to compete with one another, to dominate, fight, and when "necessary," kill one another is a manifestation of the *individuation process* at work.[29]

Stevens defends this viewpoint stating:

> Societies cannot exist without a hierarchical structure; an archetypal need

to organize ourselves collectively into a social pyramid is ingrained in our nature.

This is not a fashionable view to espouse; for the collective consensus would have us repress and deny our dominance, aggressive and proprietorial desires.[30]

Douglas draws upon a variety of sources and research materials to challenge, contradict, and debunk Stevens' position. She points out the dangers of misusing ethological research by noting how "the subjective core beneath the objectivity of science influences the world he or she sees."[31] Many of Stevens' secondary sources could be referred to as "vulgarized distortions" and "pop psychology." Douglas writes:

> These writers not only anthropomorphize, but make selective use of particular animal models and then apply them wholesale to humans. They also search around among animals and cultures, gather examples of a certain behavior pattern, ignore manifestations of opposing patterns, and then assert that what they have chosen embodies universal laws of human behavior. Not surprisingly, this behavior in turn represents, but exaggerates, the behavior of the writer's own sex, race, class and culture.[32]

She reminds us that "ethologists are still gathering the evidence for the vast variety of animal behavior."[33] Her own research has been on "animals, cultures and societies that operate under archetypal patterns of balance, harmony and interaction." By looking at the myriad interactions and balances between an organism and the world, she emphasizes, she has been impressed by the complexity of life and the "plasticity and adaptability" of humans. Her broad viewpoint allows for a variety of hypotheses to be tested and for more potentialities to be revealed.[34]

Douglas emphasizes that many of the differences between the sexes which are presumed to be innate "may rest instead on socio-cultural biases and social conditioning. These differences are likely to prove (and are proving) transitory, dependent on the time and culture."[35]

Stevens' attitude towards women damages both men and women. "It confines them to patriarchal cultural patterns on specious grounds,"[36] writes Douglas, justifying "more of the same: more duality, polarization, exploitation and war."[37] She concludes:

> The world of archetypes has far more varied and wondrous patterns and holds out far more hope than what our poor driven culture has some-

times allowed itself to envision. Stevens' view of the archetypal dimension is regressive and restrictive. By linking archetypes to a particular cultural view and backing this with faulty genetic, ethological, paleoanthropological and sociobiological arguments, Stevens, for all his eagerness, does a disservice to his original grand idea to science in general and to Jungian psychology in particular.[38]

One would hope that Jungians would be particularly aware of how easily one's subjective perspective influences what one sees in the outer world as fact or proof. Yet time and again I have heard blatant anthropomorphisms and primitive cause and effect "reasoning" from Jungians, even noted Jungians. Perhaps our scientific shadow side shows itself.

To illustrate this point I would like to examine a very important book by Marie-Louise von Franz, *Number and Time*.[39] A forerunner of such books as *The Tao of Physics* [40] and *The Dancing Wu Li Masters*,[41] it draws examples from mathematics (few of which I understood) and biology (many of which I did understand and found appalling). In Chapter Six, "The Number Three as a Rhythmic Configuration of Progressive Actualizations in Human Consciousness and the Material Realm," von Franz examines the genetic code in relationship to the *I Ching*. On page 105 she describes the sixty-four hexagrams of the *I Ching* as depicting the basic structures of the whole of existence, "signifying sixty-four possible aspects of the *unus mundus*." The eight possible combinations of triple lines (trigrams) form the individual hexagram. She then says that

One cannot escape the impression that these numerical combinations are introspective representations of fundamental processes in our psychophysical nature; indeed, the modern science of genetics has discovered that the biological genetic code of deoxyribonucleic acid (DNA) consists of *four bases*, (adenine A, thymine T, guanine G, and cytosine C) combined into three. These groups constitute the code for building up the twenty amino acids that form all our bodily proteins.

In a footnote she says "it has, however, not yet been explained how these sixty-four triplets are combined *into* the twenty amino acids" [emphasis added].

The triplets, three-letter words composed of three of any of the four nucleotide bases, do not, as von Franz states, "combine *into* amino acids." They code *for* an amino acid. For example, the triplet ATC (adenine, thymine, cytosine) is a code word for the amino acid isoleucine. When the nucleotide sequence ATC appears in a particular position on the DNA molecule, it calls for the amino acid isoleucine to be put in a particular place in a developing protein molecule. The genetic code is not for "building" *amino acids,* it is a code for making *proteins*.

Von Franz continues

> From the four bases ($4^3 =$) sixty-four different triplets come into being. Information of the genetic code is passed on by the so-called messenger RNA to the ribosomes of the cells saturated with ribonucleic acid. These cells are constructed similarly to deoxyribonucleic acid.[42]

"Cells constructed similarly to deoxyribonucleic acid (DNA)"!? What in the world does she mean? Only vaguely does she describe what the relationship *is* between cell structure and DNA. DNA is related to cell structure in much the same way that blueprints are related to a building. Any scientific mind would probably have responded with irritation, as I did, and not have continued reading. But von Franz goes on:

> The messenger RNA likewise uses triplets to form the basic figures of its code. In these genetic findings we are confronted with an exchange of "information" in living cells that corresponds exactly to the structure of the *I Ching* hexagrams.
>   This astonishing correspondence seems, more than any other evidence, to substantiate Jung's hypothesis that number regulates both psyche and matter. The same numerical model, a pattern underlying the basic processes of human memory and transmission (and thereby also the substratum of our entire conscious processes) has been discovered, first in China through an introspective examination of the unconscious psyche and then in the West through genetic research into the living cell.[43]

How can von Franz know what the "pattern underlying the basic processes of human memory" *is* and how that pattern relates to the nucleic acids, when fifteen years after *Number and Time* was written this is still one of the biggest enigmas in the scientific world? If the author demonstrated so little understanding of the way the genetic code works, how can one begin to believe her sweeping conclusions about the relationship between the *I Ching*, numbers, and the genetic code? This type of "wild" intuition, so neglectful of details, is what the scientist finds so difficult to relate to. Science is, after all, largely a discipline that unites intuitive insight with painstaking attention to detail and "reality."

In another instance, found in Chapter Seven, von Franz examines the psychophysical significance of the number four. On page 117 is a photograph of the four-cell stage of cell division following fertilization of an egg. The caption reads: "The quaternary structure of the morula, after a male gamete has met the female oozyte." The picture follows a line in the text that reads: "lastly, we must recall that the triple codes of the genetic substance DNA and memory substance RNA are built up on a *quaternio* of bases which can be combined in $4^3=64$ variations."

Clearly, the implications are that the four-cell morula stage is another biological example of the psychophysical archetypal significance of the number four. Why else would this picture be at this place in the book? The facts are that the sequence of division produces 2, 4, 8, 16, 32, 64, 128 cells, etc. Does that mean that *each* of these stages has some archetypal significance? Why is the number four singled out? There is no three-cell stage, for example. Does this mean that three has no psychophysical significance? Like Stevens, von Franz is selecting from the mass of neurological and ethological research to support a subjective viewpoint. This sort of speculation leaves a scientific mind feeling very uneasy and suspicious.

Perhaps what puts a scientist off most about Jung is his preoccupation with parapsychology. "Only ignorants don't believe in such things," Jung said in the Freeman interview, "Face to Face." Since Jung appreciated the vastness of the psyche and recognized that its exploration was still in its infancy, he felt it was foolish to approach the psyche with rigid preconceptions and theories. In his direct work with the unconscious, which involved the discovery of the structures that shape the way we perceive, think, and even theorize about the world, Jung did not limit himself to the linear, logical, and causal approach of conventional science. Jung prided himself on his empiricist approach and honored his experiences. As a result of personal experiences with synchronicity, astrology, the *I Ching*, Rhines' experiment with ESP phenomena, and nuclear physics, Jung expounded a worldview that incorporated parapsychological phenomena. This led him to put his theory of archetypes on a transcendental basis. Synchronistic and other borderline phenomena can be only partially experienced by the psyche. Most go beyond psychic experience and causal explanation. These phenomena point to a transcendental realm beyond the psyche, beyond space and time. Since one cannot approach these phenomena consciously, Jung assumed that one could only establish an acausal, that's-just-the-way-it-is orderedness to these indefinable contents. Jung felt that the archetype-as-such not only gave order to our ideas, but was completely integrated with the reality of what was nonrepresentable and nonpsychic.

Scientists might begin to understand this conception of archetypes by looking to atomic physics. Liliane Frey-Rohn offers this summary:

> Jung gave great importance to the analogous ideas and thought patterns found in physics. Just as psychologists had advanced to the borderline phenomenon of the archetype-as-such, that is, to the principle of an *a priori* orderedness and distribution of data, physicists had established certain laws of probability, related to acausal arrangements of physical factors. In order to explain various disturbances on the atomic level, caused by the presence of an observer, the physicists was forced to sacrifice the idea of causality. In the first place, problems arising from observations and from complementary circumstances (for example, the mutual exclusion of wave and particle in the theory of light) necessitated supplementing the idea of causality with statistical laws of nature. Both led to including the nonrepresentable in theoretical considerations.[44]

It is important to realize that most scientists have not been forced to grapple with the type of issues that forced nuclear physicists, over half a century ago, to abandon causality and live with the irrepresentable paradoxical. Non-atomic scientists continue to operate comfortably within the Newtonian-Cartesian worldview. Thanks to a few remarkable books written for the layman over the past decade, including Fritjof Capra's *The Tao of Physics*, *The Turning Point*,[45] and Gary Zukav's *The Dancing Wu Li Masters*, these scientists can now begin to understand nuclear physics more easily. Through such books, scientists can appreciate how Jung's acceptance of borderline phenomena (such as synchronicity) forced him to formulate a view of reality that bears many resemblances to nuclear physics.

The unknown and ultimately unknowable background of the psyche should not preclude us from constructing intellectual models and hypotheses about it. Frey-Rohn states that:

> Jung doubted that an objective intellectual judgment on the transcendental background of the psyche could ever be reached, but he always upheld the subjective value of an image or simile in so far as it conveyed the meaning and importance of the background's numinous quality.[46]

The mind can only paraphrase or approximate an ultimately unconscious nucleus of meaning. Jung concluded his speculations about matter and psyche by hypothesizing that they constitute two aspects of one and the same reality.

> The synchronicity phenomena point, it seems to me, in this direction, for they show that the nonpsychic can behave like the psychic, and vice versa, without there being any causal connection between them.[47]

I have experienced synchronicities again and again in my personal use of the *I Ching*, in the over one hundred *I Ching* consultations I have given, and in my use of the *I Ching* with my analysands. As a result of these experiences, and talks with anthropologists (whose experiences with Native American medicine men have been no different from those described in such intriguing books as *Rolling Thunder*[48] and *Black Elk Speaks*[49]), I have come to believe that synchronicity points to another level of reality. Each time I use the *I Ching* and get those highly relevant answers, my scientific *Weltanschauung* is challenged. It was in an attempt to wrestle with this split between science and synchronicity that I chose to do my thesis on the *I Ching*, synchronicity, and the theory of evolution.

Despite all my experiences with synchronicity and the *I Ching*, it was at the moment that I developed a synchronicity experiment with the *I Ching* that I was truly shaken. The reasons why I was so shaken are relevant to this paper. Bringing the power of scientific method to a very elusive Jungian topic is exciting. Science offers a systematic approach to exploration, provides a framework for gathering data, uses statistics to objectively validate, and provides a means of developing and testing hypotheses. Executing a well-designed experiment can provide a wealth of information even if the experiment "fails." Experimenting with synchronicity challenged me to honor both the subjective personal realm of the participants and the system of the *I Ching*. I could not bludgeon into these two areas in the usual scientific manner. I came to realize that many areas of interest to Jungians could be opened to research if the proper caution were exercised in designing experiments.

From my readings and experiences I have come to realize to what extent science is a belief system. A scientist puts great faith in the scientific method. Many scientists and laymen believe that given time and

the development of new techniques and theories—and enough
Einsteins—everything will be explained. A scientist can fall into the trap
of living the scientific method, of seeing and approaching life solely in
a scientific manner. It becomes crucial that the scientist be reminded,
at the very outset, what the parameters of science are. Unless one can
replicate experiments, limit variables, and objectify situations, science
cannot deal with an issue. The unusual and exceptional is weeded out
by statistical means. The power of miracles, the subjective experience
of God, love, and much else in life falls outside the domain of science.
These are just a few of the areas where a pure scientist is in danger: his
enthrallment with the scientific approach could lead him to a dry, arid,
one-sided perspective on life. Perhaps scientists should remind themselves that the Newton of their collective Newtonian worldview was one
of the last of the ancient alchemists. There was compensation, a wholeness within Newton's psyche, but the collective was denied it.

Scientists pride themselves on being open-minded, but may deceive
themselves by not realizing that they are only being open-minded *within*
the scientific framework. Parapsychological phenomena challenge that
entire framework, and thus can be very unsettling to a scientific mind
that rests upon an unconscious belief system in science. I was talking
to a friend about the *I Ching* when a former entomology advisor ap-
proached and overheard part of our conversation. "You don't really believe in that stuff, do you Dennis?" he said, and turned around and
walked away.

Demonstrations of the power and effectiveness of the scientific approach are all around us, from light bulbs to automobiles, to live trans-
missions of space shuttle flights flickering across the TV screen. Science
is convincing, especially in American society. When I ask my analysands
to record their dreams, many will say they do not dream. However, if
I tell them of scientific experiments which have proven that all people
dream, they quickly change their position to, "Well, then I must be
dreaming but I just can't remember them."

There is real hope for Jungians because science may have finally discovered that there is an unconscious! This was proclaimed in February,
1984, in a *New York Times* article entitled "New View of Mind Gives
Unconscious an Expanded Role":

> For decades mainstream research psychologists suppressed the notion

that crucial mental activity could take place unconsciously.

But now, in what one researcher calls "a silent revolution," experimental psychologists are taking the unconscious seriously in the wake of new and compelling evidence that the unconscious is the site of a far larger portion of mental life than even Freud envisioned. The main studies show that the unconscious mind may understand and respond to meaning, form emotional responses and guide most actions, largely independent of conscious awareness.

The findings imply that, despite the subjective experience of being in conscious control of feelings and thoughts, decisions and actions, people are piloted far more than they know by the unconscious mind.[50]

Maybe we can hope that scientists doing dream research will discover Jung! How many times have I read articles about dream research where the only theory mentioned is Freud's? I even heard a presentation by a university scientist doing research on the masculine and feminine aspects of the brain who did not appear to know about Jung's concepts of the anima and animus!

Currently a book by an English biochemist, Rupert Sheldrake, has been generating some interest in the scientific community. *A New Science of Life*[51] puts forth the hypothesis of morphogenic fields, claiming for example that animals tune into the experience of their ancestors. Configurations once created produce a kind of morphic resonance to recreate such configurations. The fields have no energy or spatial dimensions. The configurations created range from DNA molecules to patterns of activity in the central nervous system. Experiments are being conducted to investigate this possibility. Arden Mahlberg, a colleague of mine in Madison, Wisconsin, has conducted research suggesting that the introverted feeling function is more sensitive to these morphogenic fields.[52] Sheldrake's ideas are clearly linked to Jung's concept of the archetype-as-such and synchronicity. It has been exciting as a Jungian and as a scientist to see how Sheldrake's hypothesis has sparked interest and generated some rather novel experiments.

We may indeed be at a "turning point" in our culture, as Fritjof Capra suggests. A different *Weltanschauung* is beginning to emerge. Many new areas are opening up as brain research and body-mind issues become focused. I am convinced that Jungian concepts will play an expanded role in these and other lines of research. It becomes imperative that we as Jungians have a proper understanding and appreciation of the scientific method, as well as the sensitivity of scientists. We must bear in mind that the scientific modality is part of the shadow side of the Jungian collective. We should remind ourselves of the dangers of negative projections onto the scientific community. Scientists and Jungians stand to benefit from a better understanding and appreciation of one another's perspective as we move towards a more holistic culture, a new alchemy.

Notes

1. Dennis Merritt. 1983. "Synchronicity Experiments with the *I Ching* and Their Relevance to the Theory of Evolution." Diploma Thesis, C. G. Jung Institute, Zürich.
2. Marie-Louise von Franz. 1974. *Shadow and Evil in Fairy Tales.* Zürich: Spring Publications, pp.266-67.
3. Frank Trippett. 1981. "Aiming High in '81." *Time*, Vol.117, No. 2. January 12, 1981, p.4.
4. C.G. Jung. 1971. *Psychological Types*. In *The Collected Works of C. G . Jung*, (hereafter *CW*) Vol.6. R.F.C Hull, trans. Princeton: Princeton University Press, par.85.
5. J. Gary Sparks. 1982. *"The Wounded Finger: Anchorage for The Soul and Sense in Technology.* Diploma Thesis, C. G. Jung Institute, Zürich.
6. *Ibid.*, pp.125-138.
7. *Ibid.*, pp.115-117.
8. Marie-Louise von Franz. 1980. *The Psychological Meaning of Redemption Motifs in Fairy Tales.* Toronto: Inner City Books, p.115.
9. James Hillman. 1981. "The Imagination of Air and The Collapse of Alchemy," in *Rise and Descent, Eranos Yearbook 1981.* Vol.50. Frankfurt am Main: Insel Verlag.
10. *CW* 13, par.76.
11. C. G. Jung. 1976. *Vision Seminars*. Vol. 2. Zürich: Spring Publications, p.457.
12. Sparks, p.104.
13. *CW* 5, par.748.
14. *CW* 7, par.109.
15. Anthony Stevens. 1982. *Archetypes: A Natural History of The Self.* New York: William Morrow and Co.
16. Anthony Stevens. 1984. "Thoughts on The Psychobiology of Religion and The Neurobiology of Archetypal Experience." (Lecture).
17. J. P. Henry and P. M. Stephens. 1977. *Stress, Health and The Social Environment: a Sociobiological Approach.* New York: Springer-Verlag.
18. P. D. MacLean. 1975. "Brain Mechanisms of Primal Sexual Functions and Related Behaviour," in *Sexual Behaviour, Pharmacology and Biochemistry*. M. Sandler and G. L. Gessa, eds. New York: Raven Press, pp.1-11.
19. Stevens. *Archetypes*.
20. M. Jouvet. 1975. "The Function of Dreaming: A Neurophysiologist's Point of View," in *Handbook of Psychobiology*. M.S. Gazzaniga and C. Blakemore, eds. New York: Academic Press.

21. C. I. Smith, K. Kitahama, J. L. Valatx and M. Jouvet. 1974. "Increased Paradoxical Sleep in Mice During Acquisition of a Shock Avoidance Task." *Brain Research*, Vol.77, pp.221-230.
22. Jonathan Winson. 1978. "Loss of Hippocampal Theta Rhythm Results in Spatial Memory Deficit in The Rat." *Science.*, Vol.201, pp.160-163.
23. Stevens, lecture.
24. *Ibid.*
25. Claire Douglas. 1985. "Biology and Archetypal Theory." *The San Francisco Jung Institute Library Journal*, Vol.5, No.4, pp.1-21.
26. Stevens. *Archetypes.* p.174.
27. *Ibid.*, p.189.
28. *Ibid*, p.233.
29. *Ibid*, p.239.
30. *Ibid*, p.240.
31. Douglas, p.12.
32. *Ibid.*, p.11.
33. *Ibid.*, p.11.
34. *Ibid.*, p.21.
35. *Ibid.*, p.20.
36. *Ibid.*, p.20.
37. *Ibid.*, p.21.
38. *Ibid.*, p.21.
39. Marie-Louise von Franz. 1974. *Number and Time: Reflections Leading Towards a Unification of Psychology and Physics.* Andrea Dykes, trans. London: Rider and Co.
40. F. Capra. 1975. *The Tao of Physics.* Berkeley: Shambhala Publications.
41. G. Zukav. 1979. *The Dancing Wu Li Masters—An Overview of The New Physics.* New York: William Morrow and Co.
42. Von Franz. *Number and Time*, p.106.
43. *Ibid.*, p.106.
44. Liliane Frey-Rohn. 1976. *From Freud to Jung.* F. Engreen and E. Engreen, trans. New York: Delta; Dell Publishing Co., p.294.
45. F. Capra. 1982. *The Turning Point.* New York: Simon and Schuster.
46. Frey-Rohn, p.298.
47. *CW* 8, par.418.
48. Doug Boyd. 1974. *Rolling Thunder.* New York: Random House.
49. John G. Neihardt. 1979. *Black Elk Speaks. Being the Life History of a Holy Man of the Oglala Sioux.* Lincoln: University of Nebraska Press.
50. D. Goleman. 1984. "New View of Mind Gives Unconscious an Expanded Role." *New York Times*, Science Times. Feb.4, 1984. p.19.
51. Rupert Sheldrake. 1981. *A New Science of Life.* Los Angeles: J. P. Tarcher.
52. A. Mahlberg. 1985. "Morse Code Experiment Supports M-Field Theory." *Brain/Mind Bulletin.* Vol.10, No.12, p.1.

3

Voodoo:
Our Link with the Occult

Esther Leonard De Vos

Life, or what strikes us as most important in life, always takes place within a belief system. I think most analysts give their work, and a belief in their work, ranking priority in their lives. Perhaps it is a danger inherent in the length of time spent studying the ideas of others that we may tend to just state a general idea of what we "believe" without looking at the unconscious assumptions that may be the basis of these beliefs. To some, being a Jungian is a conviction that equals religious conviction, and like some religious convictions, it is often asserted as a matter of fact.

It is the purpose of this paper to try to conceptualize the belief system known as Voodoo as it is practiced in Haiti at the present time, and then to compare this system to some of the generally accepted beliefs identifiable within Jungian psychology.

The belief that there are invisible forces that can affect the lives and behavior of man is one of the oldest and most prevalent beliefs. In a much earlier time these invisible forces were called gods or demons. The scientist no longer claims to believe in these gods or demons, but believes the unseen forces that effects our lives and health are of a physical

33

and chemical nature. To a psychologist, these unseen forces are labeled repressed, dissociated contents of the unconscious, or if the psychologist is a Jungian, some of the forces are seen as contents of the collective unconscious and are called archetypes.

The Gestalt known as Voodoo not only believes in the presence of the invisible forces, but makes this belief its central religion. It is upon these forces that life must focus. Because the invisible forces are the central core of this system, we term the belief system of Voodoo *occult*. The word occult used in this context carries the meaning of unseen or hidden, but it may also be defined as seeking knowledge in ways other than via the rational functions — thus knowledge obtained through intuition or feeling would, in occult terms, be considered valid as well.

Voodoo is a word that is at least vaguely familiar to most of us. It is defined by Webster as "a body of primitive rites and practices, based on a belief in sorcery and in the power of charms, fetishes etc., found among natives of the West Indies and in the southern United States, and ultimately of African origin."[1] Science, on the other hand, has a somewhat more respectable definition in the same dictionary. It is a "state or fact of knowing often as opposed to intuition," and a "systematized knowledge, derived from observation, study, and experimentation carried on in order to determine the nature or principles of what is being studied."[2] In some cases science, and especially medical science, has been elevated to the status of a beneficent god, a god having special power over the lives and affairs of people and nature. With this in mind, it is easier to see that we could almost reverse the above definitions were we to look at science from outside and at Voodoo from within. My purpose is not to denigrate either science or Voodoo, but rather to set the stage for viewing Voodoo from within its own system rather than through a mist of Western rationalism.

It has been a prevalent notion that facts are those ideas one can measure and quantify. If an idea does not meet these qualifications, it becomes a "belief." By this measure, both the postulate of the presence of the collective unconscious as well as the tenets of Voodoo can be considered to be "merely belief systems" by those who scrutinize them from the outside; however, both are lived as truths by those who view from within.

Because belief systems operate at an unconscious as well as a conscious level, it is difficult to conceptualize them. These difficulties are compounded when we are confronted with an oral tradition, as we are when we study Voodoo.

We of the Judeo-Christian heritage have grown accustomed to thinking in terms of concepts; we look for religious ideals as well as for our history in the written word of the Bible, and for the most we do not remain cognizant of the fact that much of this was also once an oral tradition.

To move from precept to concept in the investigation of a belief system is tantamount to "explaining a dream." As we are aware, this will make the dream lifeless, and it then exists as a "nothing but." It has, as they say, lost something in translation. Rather, we will try to *understand* in the literal sense of the word, which is to stand under or among, and thus to comprehend. It is to our advantage to approach this ancient religion—which came to the American soil with the slave trade—as one approaches dreams, as images of something that lies in the unconscious. In doing this we will set aside the idea that it must be rational or not rational, that it is coherent or not coherent, and that it must make sense. Of course, only certain elements of the Voodoo belief system will be discussed here, and we must be consistently aware that these are only the facets that are available to our view. They do not constitute the whole.

Fundamental beliefs concerning life, the mind, and human destiny determine the actions of each individual. Each system of ideas carries with it a tendency to feel and act certain ways in a given set of circumstances.[3]

This article describes some elements of a Gestalt that incorporates into the very essence of daily living a religion, a philosophy of life, and a belief in the living presence of the ancestors. Basic to Voodoo is the belief in the existence of supernatural forces outside as well as inside the individual. The *voudun* (one who practices Voodoo) experiences Voodoo as a condition of the whole mind, feeling emotion and cognition in which a unity of perception is associated with emotion and followed immediately by a tendency to action.

First and foremost, Voodoo is concerned with the art of living. It has been described as a simple belief; it is thought to be based on a religion that existed in Africa, by conservative estimate, at least eight thousand years ago. Some say the belief may have existed in some form for as long as twenty-five thousand years. The system is based on the tradition of ancestors, who observed the universe and man and the material world as parts of that universe.[4]

Over time, certain recurring and unchangeable themes came to be considered distinguishable from the material world. Since observation and description are the foundation for correlation, this organization of experience into themes became a meaningful pattern. It is within these patterns that a principle emerged. In time the principle was perceived to be an entity separate from the material thing itself.

These principles were observed to be persistent, universal, and superior to all matter. They thus comprised an order by which man could live and to which he was subject. A principle that is immutable and powerful soon becomes identified as a force. With knowledge of these forces, it was possible to deal with the cosmos; it became understood that without these forces no life could exist.

These forces are not physical nor visible, and because of this they are referred to by the Haitian who practices Voodoo as *les invisibles*. Being invisible does not make them less real; they are considered to be true and correct. These forces can be perceived only when manifest in matter, but they are separate from the matter in which they occur.

Because man is subject to these laws, and because without them no life would exist, they took on a numinous quality, the personification of which became known as divinities. *Loa* is the Haitian word that designates one of the divinities. The term *Loa* has synonyms in the French words *saint* or *mystère*. "To worship the *loa* is to celebrate the principle, not the matter in which it may be momentarily or permanently manifest."[5]

Although each *loa* bears a separate name and has its own characteristics, in a sense each is but an aspect of one central cosmic principle. Each is differentiated merely by the emphasis with which that central principle is manifested in a separate time and place. There are said to be four hundred and one *loa*, some of which exist in natural phenomena, such as plants and trees; others are thought to reside in situations or special individuals. As in music, a *loa* is a theme which may be repeated with variations. The harmony remains and is experienced as harmony when the parts are played as one. To separate man from the nature that surrounds him is a Western idea and does not fit the configuration of Voodoo, for part of the total rationale is the connection between man and nature. "Proof" of this connection is the knowledge that the *loa* are shared by both.

There is a reciprocal relationship between the principle and the person; each *loa* partakes of the head that bears it, and at times is modified by the individual. The individual serves the *loa*, but the *loa* needs the individual to be manifest. Not only did the ancestors perceive and organize the principle that came to be called *loa*, but in some instances over the years they refined it as well. As the *loa* and person live in mutual interaction, mutations may occur with the passage of time and within the changing environment.

It is the spirit that has lived through the person of someone important, one who has served the community, who has looked after the well-being of the community, that will become *loa*. What was once seen as a principle becomes a *loa*; and thus a person who personified a *loa* may become a deity, and so the memory of the person and the purified spirit blend and remain at the disposal of the community. Voodoo is a philosophy and religion that sees the group as more important than the individual; after all, the *loa* are mutually shared by all, and thus the action of one individual will affect everyone and everything.

The knowledge of the *loa* is transmitted both by heredity and environment. When a Haitian "inherits" a *loa*, he does not understand this as separate from or distinct from his environment. To a child who has had his grandfather or any other member of his family as part of his life on a daily basis, to discern between genetic inheritance and environmental influence would seem ludicrous. The *loa* were part of the parents, they had infused them. Because *loa* serve both individuals and the community, it would follow that both by birth and by virtue of the particular environment a child would tend toward those *loa* that are near to him. The historical and social context sets what is important, but no rules determine which *loa* will infuse which person.

The voudun seems to accept this variation in the different *loa* in much the same way that we look at the psychological concept of the Self. In working with people seeking individuation, it seems as if parts of the individual unconscious were selected by an unknown agent that makes a choice of elements out of the collective unconscious. Just as all of the elements of the collective unconscious may be available to each person as part of a psychic heritage, but each individual is influenced by both individual family genetics and specific environmental forces, so it is with Voodoo. The Haitian who practices Voodoo expresses this concept by saying that·"History shapes men, and men become ancestors. When ancestors become *loa* the history of the race runs in the blood of the race as part of the psychic heritage which is passed on from generation to generation."6

In order to understand how *loa* may be modified by the lives of individuals, it is necessary to be aware of how Voodoo conceptualizes the individual. To the voudun, a person is not only composed of physical body, but also of a vital force that enters his body at birth. This vital force—which comes from, and at the time of death returns to, a cosmic pool—is known as the *gros bon ange*. It is present in every living thing. Because of it we breathe, work, and partake of life in the way animals do, but it does not provide us with what we might call the conscious awareness of Self.

In addition to the *gros bon ange*, there are other spiritual forces that enter the body at the time of birth. These are the *loa* previously discussed. Most prominent among them is the *petit bon ange*. The presence of the *petit bon ange* makes an individual the particular person he or she is. The *petit bon ange* allows one to think, analyze, synthesize, and choose one behavior over another. It is the spiritual force that infuses an individual with his particularly human quality. It is what we might refer to as "soul" or "psyche."

When a person dies, the *petit bon ange* does not return to a cosmic pool as does the *gros bon ange*; rather it is reincarnated into another individual. In order to understand how this happens, we must keep in mind that the person does not possess the *petit bon ange* nor does the *petit bon ange* possess the person. The relationship is reciprocal; one acts in response to the other. Thus the person experiences meaning through the *petit bon ange*, yet his or her actions simultaneously affect the *petit bon ange*. It is said that after sixteen incarnations the *petit bon ange* may appear before Dhamballa, the great serpent of the sky, and if pure enough it becomes a *loa* and is no longer incarnated into another person. In contemporary language, we would say that when the ego is purified it becomes spirit.

A person must serve the spirits with which he is infused, yet he may also call upon the *loa* for help. He may wish to ask for help in the enterprises of everyday life. Most often he seeks assistance in times of distress and disharmony, especially illness. It is the *houngan*, what we might call the Voodoo shaman, who knows how to call upon the *loa*. There must be a peristyle, a special outdoor area set aside for invocation and worship, and used for no other purpose. Fitting our idea of *temenos*, the Greek term for sacred precinct, the peristyle is a holy place. It must be decorated in a manner pleasing to the particular *loa* to be invoked, and the direction through which that *loa* will choose to enter must be known. Most often the *loa* will enter through the *poteau-mitan*, a center post which represents the cosmological axis—an idea common in shamanism. The houngan must draw the particular *vever,* a mandala-like drawing or symbol, that is specific to the *loa* in question. He must know the language, color, food preference, and special drink of the *loa*. These divinatory techniques necessary for calling a *loa* are known only to the initiated.

Occasionally, a person is possessed by a *loa*. The *loa* attaches itself to the person's *petit bon ange* for a short while, bringing about what is known as the possession crisis phenomenon. The possession crisis itself is brief in duration, usually lasting from five to eight minutes, and manifests itself in three distinct phases. The first stage is hyperventilation, during which the person remains conscious but experiences distortions in perceptions, including hallucinations and loss of equilibrium. This stage in effect identifies *which* individual will be possessed. The second phase follows immediately, and is typified by psychomotor agitation. Since the individual is possessed by a particular *loa*, his behavior at this time will necessarily be characteristic. This helps other vouduns to identify the *loa* in question. During this phase, consciousness is lost. The third stage is marked by the collapse of the person possessed, after which he soon regains consciousness. There is always amnesia for the duration of the possession crisis.[8]

In contrast to analysis, where individuality is retained and developed, the possession crisis ceremony brings people together in a common ritual with a prescribed goal. The individual abandons himself to the group in a kind of ecstasy or act of surrender. Something greater than the individual emerges; an energy resembling that generated by mob action—though in this case the energy released is channeled toward to positive goal of healing.

It should be kept in mind that for the voudun, possession is a fact of life he has observed since his early childhood. It is considered normal, even beneficent. The ceremony itself could be described as a healing ceremony. The spirits being called are not strangers; they are part of everyday life, and they are being asked to make their presence felt.

It would not be straining credibility to propose that the contents of the collective unconscious are experienced as *loa* by those whose belief system is Voodoo, and as archetypes by those whose belief system is analytical psychology. If this assumption is permitted, possession becomes analogous to the experience of an archetypal dream, a dream in which the complex appears in personified form. In both possession and dreams a person is presented with the image of a psychic situation which is strongly emotional. In neither case, dreaming or possession, does the ego stand in the way of the experience.

Jung wrote:

> The image is a condensed expression of the psychic situation as a whole, and not merely, nor even predominantly, of unconscious contents pure and simple. It undoubtedly does express unconscious contents, but not the whole of them, only those that are momentarily constellated. This constellation is the result of the spontaneous activity of the unconscious on the one hand and of the momentary conscious situation on the other, which always stimulates the activity of relevant subliminal material and, at the same time, inhibits the irrelevant.[9]

The invocation of a *loa* during a possession crisis encourages such a constellation both because the situation itself creates an expectation and because the symbols used are powerful ones.

Voodoo is more magical than meditative, and it thus differs from those religions and healing practices most familiar to us. The possession crisis ceremony is therefore magical in atmosphere, and adheres to that principle of magic which brings something into focus and directs it toward a desired end. As in all magic, what is visible may hide what lies behind — in this instance, often a drug derived from a particular plant or leaf. The chosen plant or leaf is part of the houngan's repertoire, but it is believed that the choice is dictated by the *loa* and that the plant will prove to be the correct medicine needed for healing.

During the possession crisis, the *petit bon ange* is temporarily superseded by another *loa*, but the *petit bon ange* may also be altered by other circumstances. It may be manipulated, for instance, by another, more powerful person, in what is termed the zombie phenomenon. The zombie state is also induced by a drug — a fact excessively emphasized by the voudun as society's right to punish its wrongdoers.[10] The *petit bon ange* may also wander from the body during anesthesia or drug-induced states, or even deep sleep. It is to wandering of the *petit bon ange* that the voudun ascribes his feeling vaguely "out of sorts" when he is abruptly awakened before he has completed a normal sleep period.

Voodoo is much older and is considered more "primitive" than the belief system of the analyst, yet the presence of invisible forces plays an important role in each. It is the analyst, who places archetypal theory at the center of his practice, who will gain most from the comparison of the two belief systems.

Although the twenty volumes of Jung's *Collected Works* constitute the underpinnings of analytical psychology, as one searches in them for Jung's basic theory, one is confronted with a series of ideas and observations that often appear to lack cohesion and, at times, to be contradictory. Many of Jung's observations were first presented orally at seminars or lectures. Once again we are faced with the problems that arise when an oral tradition becomes a written one.

Jung denied that he had described all the contents of the psyche or that he had postulated an all-inclusive theory. It has been the task of those who study the ideas of Jung to integrate and organize them. Jolande Jacobi made strides in this direction in 1939 when she wrote *The Psychology of C.G. Jung*. Presenting Jung's theory, she selected three principles which Jung himself stated as concise presentations of his psychological theory.[11]

The first principle concerns the nature and structure of the psyche. The description of the psyche as tripartite is familiar to all analytical psychologists. I do not know to what extent the houngan conceptualizes the psyche topographically or whether he does so at all. But just as the analysand does not see our conceptual divisions and seeks analysis unaware of the effect of the unconscious on daily life, so too the voudun lives within a Gestalt without needing to describe or to conceptualize it.

The second principle is the recognition of certain "laws of psychic processes and forces." There are apparent similarities between this principle and the *loa*, as previously mentioned. The living presence of the *loa* is central to the voudun: no life is present without the *loa*. Those forces are not abstract principles, but personalities with which the voudun must constantly deal. The *loa*, if deprived of their voice or cheated of the use of their energy, weep and threaten to leave. The most obvious divergence between the two systems, especially for those who take a more empirical view, arises over whether the forces can exist outside the psyche. This possibility is not entirely foreign to analytical psychology. It was suggested by Jung in the following passage, written in 1934:

> The nixie is an even more instinctive version of a magical feminine
> being whom I call the *anima*. Moralizing critics will say that these figures
> are projections of soulful and emotional states and are nothing but worth-
> less fantasies. One must admit that there is a certain amount of truth
> in this. But is it the whole truth? Is the nixie really nothing but a prod-
> uct of moral laxity? Were there not such beings long ago, in an age when
> dawning human consciousness was still wholly bound to nature? Surely
> there were spirits of forest, field, and stream long before the question
> of moral consciousness ever existed. An unlimited amount of what we now
> feel to be an integral part of our psychic being disports itself merrily for
> the primitive in projections ranging far and wide.[12]

According to Jung, the word "projection"

> is not really appropriate, for nothing has been cast out of the psyche;
> rather, the psyche has attained its present complexity by a series of acts
> of introjection. Its complexity has increased in proportion to the despiritu-
> alization of nature.[13]

Marie-Louise von Franz, in her recent *Projection and Recollection in
Jungian Psychology*, (1980) addresses this same question:

> The spirits that rule over animals and plants are probably the oldest
> forms in which archetypal contents were imagined; among the Bushmen
> and Australian aborigines — that is, in cultures that have remained espe-
> cially close to their origins — they are actual gods. In contrast to the up-
> per and lower spirits, they are localized in the surrounding world of nature
> and are not separated into "light" and "dark."[14]

In the same work, she states: "Hence Jung, in his early work, assumed
that such spirits were nothing more than the embodiment of projected
images, approximate representations of the father complex, the mother
complex, and so on." Jung later revised this opinion and was no longer
sure that spirits were only personal images, possessing no separate reality of their own. Von Franz tells us that "This opens up the whole question of the transpsychic reality immediately underlying the psyche." Jung
himself writes that

> The so-called reality of matter is attested primarily by our sense-
> perception, while belief in spirit is supported by psychic experience.[15]

The theory of synchronicity also leads our thoughts in this direction.[16] Whether verifiable evidence can be found to support the idea that forces may exist outside of the human psyche remains a moot point.

In Voodoo, as in analytical psychology, there is a belief in the presence of what we call the collective unconscious. In their individual ways, both systems maintain Jung's formulation that

> The collective unconscious contains the whole spiritual heritage of mankind's evolution, born anew in the brain structure of every individual.[17]

The use in analytical psychology of the word "soul" or "spirit" (especially when capitalized) corresponds most closely to the *petit bon ange* of Voodoo. Jacobi, paraphrasing Jung, writes that

> By "intelligent" we mean the power of conscious thought and understanding, the purely rational side of the individual. "Spirit" is to be taken as a faculty which pertains to the realm of consciousness but also has a natural bond with the unconscious; it leads primarily to meaningful artistic, ethical-religious accomplishments, to the form of insights and utterances, but it can also lend definite coloration to thoughts and judgments as well as emotional attitudes. Spirit in this sense comprises both intellect and soul; it forms a bond between them and is a meaningful "sublimation" of both, it is a formative principle constituting the contrary pole to the unformed, instinctual, biological nature of man, thereby sustaining the continual tension of opposites on which our psychic life is based.[18]

Again, using the words of Jolande Jacobi: "The word 'soul' has a specific meaning in Jungian terminology; here we use it in the sense of a definite, circumscribed functional complex which might be characterized as a kind of inner personality." I would also add that it is the "subject" to which the ego-consciousness of the individual is related, in the same way as to an outward object. In Jung's definition, the subject "conceived as 'the inner' object, is the unconscious. The same autonomy that very often characterizes the outer attitude is claimed also by the inner attitude."[19]

The loss of soul, or lack of spirit, has already been described as the "zombie-like" phenomenon. All of us have experienced people who appear to be empty shells. These people carry on a semblance of social life, maintain a job, do the external tasks required of them, but seem to have little connection with the vital force we feel comes from the unconscious. In the language of the voudun, they have lost possession of their *petit bon ange.*

Another example indicating a correspondence between the Jungian and the Voodoo systems of classifying the contents of the collective unconscious is the concept of the *Mait-tête,* or dominant *loa.*

In Voodoo, each person is said to have a *Mait-tête,* a *loa* which is literally described as the "master of the head." It is the dominant *loa,* not in the sense that it controls the person, but rather that it is the *loa* which most nearly matches the identity of the person who possesses it.[20] This *loa,* in other words, confers the favor of its presence on the person who is most sympathetic to it. *Mait-tête,* a somewhat ambiguous phrase, refers to something between our words "soul" and "ego." It is the personality type on which a person projects his soul. In analytical psychology it would be considered the dominant archetype in a person's life.

Dr. Adolf Guggenbühl-Craig, lecturing in Zürich on the topic "Archetypes in Everyday Life,"[21] pointed out that by listening to the usage of words in conversations and dreams one could see each individual's tendency towards a particular archetype. For instance, a person living under the warrior archetype might sprinkle his conversation with words such as "challenge," "win," "conquer," and might view each undertaking in a competitive light. He might be a person who, in common parlance, it said to exhibit "type-A behavior." Similarly, a voudun might be said to be living under a particular *loa,* his *Mait-tête.* In both systems the dominance of one does not negate the presence of other archetypes or *loa.*

There are numerous parallels between the *loa* and the archetypes. To mention only a few, the *Loa Legba* is described as the *loa* of the crossroads, and he bears a resemblance to the archetype of Hermes. The goddess of love, Erzulie, is described as a muse of beauty, and seems to fit the description of Aphrodite.[22]

Both analytical psychology and Voodoo believe that "invisible forces" are at work within the human psyche. Looking now at the complex theory, it becomes clear that both systems also believe that these forces can possess the individual, or as Jung stated, "possession can be formulated as identity of the ego-personality with a complex."[23]

A complex, with its given emotional component, has a tendency to form a personality or partial personality — or a "splinter psyche," as Jung called it. In each person's psychology are figures that seem to have a definite life of their own, the animus and the anima being those most often identified.

It is the collective nature of the god or goddess in Voodoo which makes different people act similarly when possessed. In analytical psychology, we observe how women possessed by the animus or men by the anima lose their unique individuality and act in more generalized ways. This tendency of autonomy shows itself above all in affective states.

Although the word "possession" is sprinkled liberally throughout Jung's works, it is a word that is not commonly found in scientific literature today. The compartmentalization of Western scientific and religious ideas is apparent in the usage of the word "possession," which has been relegated to religious contexts only.

Possession in Christianity is not dissimilar from possession in Voodoo, except that in Christianity the only possession sought is by the Holy Ghost: all other possessions are considered works of the devil.

The word "possession" may not be part of our accepted psychological vocabulary—except in quotes from Jung—but the phenomenon itself seems to be alive and well, functioning under other names. In the main body of psychiatric and psychological literature, for instance, it is easy to find articles which describe obsession, few or none which describe possession. According to Webster, the words "possession" and "obsession" have similar meanings. The word "obsession" originally meant "to be under the influence of an evil possession." In *The Comprehensive Textbook of Psychiatry*, the prestigious psychiatric textbook edited by Kaplan and Sadork, the history of obsession is traced back to an account of possession recorded in the fifteenth century. The text reiterates Janet's 1893 postulate that when a pathological diminution of mental energy takes place, the result is a disintegration of the higher functions which permit the lower, more subsidiary functions to take over.[24] This explanation is the often-cited *abaissement du niveau mental* with which any reader of Jung's *Collected Works* is already familiar.

Many examples of modern day "possession" could be cited, but one example will suffice here. Currently, it is fashionable to label behavior "obsessive-compulsive," or to call a pattern an "eating disorder": both these terms are considered diagnoses in the DSM III (*Diagnostic & Statistical Manual*, third edition). Possession, on the other hand, is considered neither a diagnosis nor a valued description in many circles. However, Heinz E. Lehman, in an article entitled, "Voodoo and Other Possession States," suggests an instance in which possession can clearly be considered a possibility. Western culture is spawning its own idiopathic disorders, he speculates. "The aesthetic-cosmetic publicity-oriented feeling in Western culture typified by the slim-is-beautiful axiom probably underlies the almost explosive upsurge of anorexia nervosa and bulimia"[25] This statement, under the heading of "possession," is not a novel idea to those who see behavior, emotions, and images within the context of the complex theory.

I would like to suggest that a spirit of the times which calls for slenderness at all costs can become an "invisible force" in the environment as well as in the psyche. The woman who lacks connection with her soul (here used in Jolande Jacobi's sense, as a circumscribed functional complex which might be characterized as a kind of "inner personality") is susceptible to possession by this spirit or invisible force. In other words, when her life experiences make it difficult for a woman to have contact with her feminine soul, she becomes vulnerable to the spirits that exists in the environment, and this may be tantamount to a possession.

In 1916, Jung wrote that "Analytical treatment could be described as a readjustment of psychological attitudes achieved with the help of the doctor."[26] I believe the Haitian houngan might describe his work in somewhat the same way.

Many similarities between the two systems have already been described. However, when we come to the third principle mentioned in Jacobi's work, "the practical application of Jung's theory," we find major differences. The goal of the houngan's and analyst's work might share similarities, but the processes used to attain those goals are quite different.

There are as many variations in the practice of analytical psychology as there are analysts in practice, but the generally accepted goal of analysis is individuation gained through insight. In Voodoo the person who seeks help does not expect or work towards insight. It is the prescribed emotional experience that brings about his healing.

Dr. Douyon, a psychiatrist practicing in Port-au-Prince, Haiti, has made a lifelong study of the practice of Voodoo. He states that the function of the possession crisis is to discharge ego dystonic feelings and guilt: possession is ego-supporting and tends to bring about a reorganization of emotions.[27] The Voodoo belief system encourages this giving up of conscious control for a brief time—the ego is completely set aside and trust is placed in the houngan. The goodwill and shared belief of the group, as well as the knowledge that if the god is propitiated (hence favorite food, drink, dress, etc.), there will be an experience that is temporally limited and that will bring about a reunification of the personality, and sustain the individual throughout the crisis.

The stage is set by the sacredness of the place and the drawing of the *vever*. Prolonged dancing to a hypnotic drum follows, and it has been hypothesized that this experience, by resulting in self-induced stress which activates the body's endorphins and endogenous immune responses, is curative to those involved.

Magic can be described as *not* knowing; the one acted upon by magic is *experiencing* a power. Seeking knowledge is not his purpose. Dynamism is the theory that force or energy is basic to all phenomena, and it follows that there are persons capable, in certain circumstances, of activating these forces, of concentrating the cosmic forces. Whether this is totally different from "constellating the healer archetype" will be left to the speculation of the individual reader.

In Voodoo, the person capable of manipulating the power is the houngan. The houngan has often been maligned and, as in any field, there are no doubt houngans who are charlatans; however, the main function and life work of the houngan is to heal. In order to qualify for the vocation of houngan, special talents and a long period of training are required. Certain tendencies must be identified before the training is undertaken. "Sometimes it is possible to know from the cradle. This may be indicated by how the babe drinks milk, how he takes the mother's tit in the mouth; at age four or five how he deals with problems and with others. By the age of sixteen or seventeen, leadership qualities are emerging."[28] How the young man deals with his education is also significant.

The training period may last as long as five years. The master houngan passes along his formal knowledge to an apprentice and then, for several more years, supervises the work of the apprentice. When the apprentice has made the expected progress, he is initiated and allowed to begin to practice on his own. It is assumed, however, that he will return to his teacher, or turn to others, for further guidance. The formal training is said to be only the beginning, the opening of the door. Learning continues and the houngan grows in knowledge over time and with experience.[29]

The parallels between the houngan's training and that of the analyst is obvious. Only recently have training institutes begun to replace the apprenticeship aspects of the analyst's training.

One of the functions of the houngan is to interpret dreams. He must understand his own and be able to help others understand theirs. The dream is believed to present symbols for interpretation, though whether the word "symbol" means the same to the houngan as it does to the analyst is doubtful. One example of a dream symbol interpretation, when clarification is sought, is that "a tree might represent a forest."

In Voodoo, dreams are not considered to be entirely unconscious in origin. This may be explained by the Voodoo belief that the psyche is not divided between the conscious and the unconscious. There are believed to be two different kinds of dreams. One variety is meant to be forgotten; the other is to be remembered and told. If one does not find another person to whom to tell such a dream, it must be told to oneself. The dreams to be told are vivid dreams and it is often difficult for the voudun to distinguish them from real life or from a vision. Life in the hours that follow the dream relates to the dream, and, it is believed, "the dream will tell you how to conduct your life"—what you are or are not permitted to do.

In Voodoo, illnesses and accidents are believed to occur when basic laws are broken. An imbalance has occurred and it is necessary to restore the now-lost equilibrium. One houngan describes living in imbalance as trying to swim upstream; "the houngan takes your hand and puts you in water where the current is less strong and the swimming is easier."[30]

The goal of analysis is defined as follows by Murray Stein:

> Jungian analysis takes place within a dialectical relationship between two persons, analyst and analysand, and has for its goal the analysand's coming to terms with the unconscious; the analysand is meant to gain insight into the specific unconscious structures and dynamics that emerge during analysis, and the structures underlying ego-consciousness are meant to change in their dynamic relation to other, more unconscious structures and dynamics.[31]

What the individual analyst does to bring about this change varies from case to case. There is little doubt that a knowledge of unconscious forces is essential to both houngan and analyst. Within Voodoo, forces are believed to have an existence separate from the psyche; they are manifested through the psyche. Analysts believe the archetypal core of a complex will remain unchanged, but they avoid making statements about whether the forces within individuals have an independent life of their own.

Armanda Favazza tells us that "true shamans possess a high tolerance for unconscious material and primary process thinking, and they have an unusual ability to recognize and organize unconscious needs and concerns, both in themselves and in their cultural group."[32] If we accept her definition, both houngan and analyst could call themselves shamans.

Are we analysts, shamans, artists, or scientists? If a belief system helps to determine certain modes of behavior, then the system of ideas within which we see our profession affects the way we practice our profession and live our lives.

Much of the material has been gathered from attendance at conferences sponsored by the Neuropsychiatric Institute of Southern California; Folk Healing and the Occult; and from private conversations with Lamarque Douyon, M.D., Director, Centre de Psychiatrie et de Neurologie, Port-au-Prince, Haiti; and with Max G. Beauvoir, Le Péristyle de Mareani, Port-au-Prince, Haiti. The material concerning the belief system of Voodoo, unless specifically noted, is a generalization from these lectures and conversations as well as readings from anthropological works. Every effort has been made to avoid distortion, but one's own belief system necessarily "selects" a point of view.

Notes

1. Webster's New 20th Century Dictionary. The World Publishing Co., p. 2050.
2. Webster's, *op.cit.*, p.1622.
3. Richard Burton Onions, *The Origin of European Thought.* New York: Arno Press, 1973, p.83.
4. Conversation with Max Beauvoir, Houngan, November 1984.
5. Maya Deren, *Divine Horseman, The Living God of Haiti.* New York: McPherson and Co., 1983, p.89
6. Deren, *op. cit.*, p.71
7. Material from lecture by Lamarque Douyon, M.D., International Conference of Neuropsychiatric Institute, 1984.
8. Douyon, *op. cit.*
9. C. G. Jung, *Collected Works*, Vol. VI. Princeton: Princeton University Press, 1971, par.745.
10. Lecture by Max Beauvoir, 1984.
11. Jolande Jacobi, *The Psychology of C. G. Jung.* London: Routledge and Kegan Paul, 1942, p.1.

12. C. G. Jung, *CW* , Vol. IX-1, par.53.
13. *Ibid.* par.54
14. Marie-Louise von Franz, *Projection and Recollection in Jungian Psychology*. La Salle and London: Open Court, 1982, p.104.
15. C. G. Jung, Vol. VIII , par.251.
16. *Ibid.*, Chapter 7.
17. *Ibid.*, par.342.
18. Jolande Jacobi, *op cit*, p.5.
19. *Ibid.*
20. Deren, *op. cit.*, p.31.
21. Lecture heard in 1981; general idea quoted from memory.
22. Deren, *op. cit.*, Chapter III.
23. C. G. Jung, Vol. IX-1, par.220.
24. John C. Nemish, M.D., "Obsessive-Compulsive Disorders," *Comprehensive Textbook of Psychiatry*, Vol. I. Harold I. Kaplan, M.D., and Benjamin J. Sadock, eds. Baltimore/London: Williams and Willkins, 1925, p.905.
25. Heinz E. Lehman, "Unusual Psychiatric Disorders, Atypical Psychoses, and Brief Reactive Psychoses," *Textbook of Psychiatry. op cit*, p.1236.
26. C.G. Jung, Vol. VIII, par.142.
27. Lamarque Douyon, M.D., *op. cit.*
28. Raymond Prince, M.D., lecture, Neuropsychiatric Conference, November 1984.
29. Personal communication with Max Beauvoir, September 1985.
30. Max Beauvoir, *op. cit.*
31. Murray Stein, *Jungian Analysis*. LaSalle: Open Court Publishing, 1982, p.29.
32. Armanda R. Favazza, M.D., M.Ph., "Anthropology and Psychiatry," *Textbook of Psychiatry, op. cit*, p.260

4

Stages of Life as Levels
of Consciousness in the Analyst

June Singer

The wisdom of the consensus informs us that life begins with birth and ends with our death. But is this really true, or is it simply what we, in our society, have agreed upon? When you reflect on this "truism" in the light of the current controversy about abortion, it immediately begins to fall apart. Right-to-lifers say "life begins at conception." Some pro-choice advocates place the beginning of human life somewhere between the end of the first trimester of pregnancy and the date of birth. Most biological scientists take the position of the anti-abortionists as to when life begins. In Australia, where I spent last summer, the remnants of a people's consensual wisdom are forty thousand years old. The Aboriginal is perhaps the oldest living mythology on earth, and fast disappearing. There, a child is born of a spirit that first appears in dreams, even before the woman is pregnant (Isaacs, 1980).

An old Jewish legend tells us that when it is decided on high that a child will be born, the Lord sends one of his angels to bring down a soul from "beyond the stars" and to implant it in the womb of the pregnant woman. Only when the soul is firmly implanted — and this often takes a bit of doing because some souls are reluctant to leave

51

Paradise—can life be said to exist (Ginzberg, 1938, pp.55-59).

Other cultures describe life's beginning in different ways. Each believes its consensual version to be *the* truth, even as scientists and lay people in our own generation here in the Western world insist that the way they see it is the way it is. I am convinced that we see what we believe. So, with this brief introduction, I want to look at what Jung believed about the stages of life and what, consequently, he saw. Jung began his essay "The Stages of Life" with these words:

> To discuss the problems connected with the stages of human development is an exacting task, for it means nothing less than unfolding a picture of psychic life in its entirety from the cradle to the grave (1969, par.749).

Yet Jung severely limited the scope of his task at that time. He identified four stages of life. The first consists of infancy and childhood. The second is youth, beginning with the years just after puberty and ending with middle life which, he said, begins between the thirty-fifth and fortieth year. The third stage spans the period from midlife until the onset of old age, and the fourth or final stage lasts from old age until death. Of the first and fourth stages, he had little to say.

Jung characterized each stage by its "problems." Problems arise in the conflicts between instinct and consciousness. "It is just man's turning away from instinct—his opposing himself to instinct—" says Jung, "that creates consciousness. Instinct is nature and seeks to perpetuate nature, whereas consciousness can only seek culture or its denial." (1969, par.750)

Childhood, according to Jung, is characterized by unconsciousness and trust in nature. To watch small children in the process of becoming conscious is to see in the early years something that is at best sporadic, "like single lamps or lighted objects in the far-flung darkness." He goes on to say that

> In the childish stage of consciousness there are as yet no problems; nothing depends upon the subject, for the child itself is still wholly dependent upon its parents. It is as though it were not yet completely born, but were still enclosed in the psychic atmosphere of its parents. Psychic birth, and with it the conscious differentiation from the parents, normally takes place only at puberty, with the eruption of sexuality. . . . Until this period is reached, the psychic life of the individual is governed largely by instinct, and few or no problems arise (1969, par.756-757).

Conscious problems, Jung says, fill out the second and third stages of life, while in the last stage, extreme old age, "we descend again into that condition where, regardless of our state of consciousness, we once more become something of a problem for others. Childhood and extreme old age have one thing in common: submersion in unconscious psychic happenings." And he concludes his essay by saying, "Childhood and old age are the stages of life without any conscious problems, for which reason I have not taken them into consideration here." (1969, par.795). I cannot agree that, because in childhood and old age we are closer to the unconscious, we are somehow less conscious. To my mind, we are fully conscious at those times, but our consciousness has a different quality than it has in youth and middle-life.

I would like to propose four stages of life that do not correspond precisely with Jung's; nevertheless, they do comprise a life-cycle. I see these four life-stages not as fixed in time, but rather as levels of consciousness, and especially as levels of consciousness in the analyst. I call these stages: the non-personal stage, the pre-personal stage, the personal or ego stage, and the transpersonal stage. A cycle is defined as "an interval of time during which one sequence of a regularly recurring succession of events or phenomena is completed" (Webster, 1961). The Great Treatise on the *I Ching* says,

> We learn by observing the beginnings and endings of life that birth and death form one recurrent cycle. Birth is the coming forth into the world of the visible; death is the return into the regions of the invisible. Neither of these signifies an absolute beginning or an absolute ending (Wilhelm/Baynes, 1976, p.294).

In this sense, any one of these stages could be the first or the last, depending upon where we choose to begin our exploration.

Jungian analysts who daily reflect upon the conduct and meaning of their lives have an opportunity to experience these stages of life as levels of consciousness. We hear so much these days about child development, adult development. Much of this is useful information, and yet there are times when the analyst must put aside all the "received knowledge." Because we have learned to look at each person with fresh eyes, with what Zen Buddhists call "beginner's mind," we understand what it is to put aside our preconceptions and to stay with just what is before us. With the passing of years we will have learned to pay less attention to what people say about human development and more attention to what we know from our own experience as analysts and our reflections upon those experiences. Surely, we try to keep to an attitude of lightly suspended judgment when we meet our clients. We ask questions, of course, about their early memories.

But do we do this for ourselves? Do we ask the deep questions with an attitude of lightly suspended judgment? I don't mean when we were in training, or when we were going to analysis one or two or more times a week. I mean now, in our quiet moments of reflection. Do we allow our consciousness to seep down into the nearly forgotten repository of pre-verbal memories, the early pre-personal stage of our own life before the ego had coalesced, and recollect the seeds that only later germinated?

I would like to ask you to imagine that you are in utter and complete darkness. You are in the darkness of the void. It is the *prima materia* of alchemy. It is the blackness of *chaos confusum.* It is the holy place of all endings and beginnings. Creation has not yet occurred for you. There are no shapes, no forms. My voice is only to remind you of what you knew before you were born, and perhaps even before you were conceived.

Winds rush around in the wilderness of nothingness. You are like a seed under the ground and under the winter snows. You are like a stone under the water of the deepest fjord. You are like the ashes of a body that has been cremated and then flung out to sea. You are like a breath that has been dissipated in the atmosphere. You are an imaginary rope-dancer hanging in empty space, having departed from life and not yet having been born. You are immersed in the primal sea, the pleroma, the collective unconscious. But no, you are not you, you are not even yourself. You exist only *in potentia.* There is the possibility that you may exist, but this possibility has not yet become manifest.

And yet, it is all there, waiting to unfold. Wrapped in the darkness of the mystery of Life is the possibility of being. It exists in the residue of all the lives that have ever been lived, human and animal, plant, and every living thing. Individuals of every species have, in the past, cast off their earthly forms and shed their identities. They have been annihilated. There is no longer any trace of what they once were. From matter, they have been transformed into energy. They exist as elementary particles dancing in infinite space. You always knew that you were there divergence between the two systems, as we count it in this world. But you have forgotten.

You are like the soul that was called forth, according to the old myth, by the angel, to take up residence in the womb of a woman living on the planet Earth. Reluctantly you left your eternal home. When the angel shut you up in the womb, she sat before the door all night to make sure you did not escape. In the morning she came and called you forth to travel with her. She showed you the seven heavens, with the souls of the righteous enjoying the music of lutes and celestial song, and she told you that if you lived a good life this would be your destination. Then she shut you up again in the womb for another night. The next day, she took you on another trip, this time through the seven hells where she showed you the tortures of the damned. She told you that this would be your fate if you lived an evil life. And on the third day she came again and brought you out and showed you what your life would be life on earth, who your parents would be, your sisters and brothers, where you would go to school, where you would travel, where you would live, whom you would love, whom you would marry, your children, your occupation and, at last, your death. And then she shut you up and sealed the womb for nine months.

Now the time has come for you to be born. The angel comes to announce that it is time to leave the place that has become so comfortable for you. As a matter of fact, it has felt rather cramped and crowded lately, but still you are unwilling to leave it for the world outside. But the angel insists. Still, you refuse. The angel strikes you hard on the nose, causing the sparks to fly. In that painful moment you forget everything she has shown you. You come forth kicking and screaming into a world that is alien and strange.

Return to where you were before the fantasy began. It is light here. Sometimes, at odd moments, you will remember bits of what you once knew. You will feel that you have been in these places before. A face is familiar. You recognize feelings of love and fear and you know what they are. But it is vague and ephemeral for the most part.

Being born is not the beginning. It is a new stage in the cycle, an interval in the ongoing process of Life that has neither beginning nor ending, although individual lives may be said to begin and end. Your emergence is simply an event, one of many in Nature's scheme to fulfill her own purposes. In Wordsworth's words, you come, "trailing clouds of glory," for "Our birth is but a sleep and a forgetting" (1918, p.628).

After the dim silence of the predawn, the sun pierces the horizon like the cry of an infant at birth. The pre-personal stage begins. Pre-personal means the stage before the ego has been fully formed. It spans the time from birth to puberty, and sometimes extends into early adolescence. The pre-personal stage begins with almost no awareness of the difference between self and other. It continues until generally there exists a solid sense of individual identity, sexual differentiation, and a readiness to separate from the family milieu. For the person who may someday become an analyst, there may come experiences during this period which — in hindsight — will be understood as having had a role in directing the individual toward that particular path. This is the "morning of life."

In the transition from the pre-personal to the personal or ego stage, the late adolescent struggles with issues around giving up childish ways and adopting adult patterns of behavior. There are pulls in both directions: pressures of jobs or education, striving to be attractive to potential or actual sexual partners, gaining status among peers. All this requires carefully prescribed behaviors. While everything on the outside motivates toward conformity and social acceptance, a counterbalance often arises from within. Moving out into the world, with its requirements for thinking and planning, almost calls for a repression of inwardness, of the introverted intuitive and feeling functions. Yet for some at this time of life there is a sort of low keyed, almost embarrassed or not-too-serious preoccupation with dreams, religion or philosophy. People in this transitional phase may nurture an unoutspoken interest in occultism, magic and esoteric cults or the more mystical aspects of traditional religions. They may be interested also in astrology, extrasensory perception, body-mind interactions, hypnotism and non-traditional healing methods. So these not entirely respectable areas of life exist in the shadow of the mainstream disciplines to which the young adult is subjected.

I am thinking also now of Jung who, while in medical school, also occupied himself with attending seances and observing the trance medium who was later to become the subject of his doctoral dissertation. Perhaps it is well for us, as analysts, to reflect upon how we handled the play between the pressures to conform to the collective and the upward surgings of archetypal material from the deeper levels of the unconscious at this transitional phase in our lives — and what the implications of this struggle may have been for our subsequent work.

The personal or ego stage begins at the high noon of our lives. This is the time so dear to the ego psychologist, indeed, to most psychologists, for here their therapeutic skills are most often employed. It is a time of understanding intellectually, a time of problem solving, of goal-setting and planning, of making life work. It is a time when people want things to be open and clear. They want answers. They want to accomplish what they can out in the world and in their personal and family lives. Mind-body integration is part of this , too, for many people. This can mean anything from following a fitness regime to aiming for an active and fulfilling sex life. The more esoteric concerns of late adolescence have been but aside. There simply "isn't time" because there is so much to do in the adult world of career and mate and home and in the acquisition of status and possessions. As the zenith of this stage it is not altogether clear whether the so-called "successful" person controls his or her own life or if the life style controls the person.

This personal stage can, but does not necessarily, end at thirty-five or forty where Jung placed the start of the second half of life. Some people remain stuck in their ego-bounded frames indefinitely, or until they simply cannot maintain these borders, which then slowly crumble away. In the heat of the day when everything moves at a fever pitch, we often do not realize that the shadows are beginning to lengthen.

I use the word "shadows" not only in the generic sense, but also in the Jungian sense, to suggest the shadowy quality that ushers in the transition to that stage of life which I am calling transpersonal. What has been repressed or hidden in the process of achieving social acceptance, now begins to find its voice. More often than not it is a shadow problem that forces one's attention to turn from life's accomplishments (or failures to accomplish) to the darker side, where something was not done rightly, where the ego has not had its will, where there has been a shock, or disappointment in oneself or in others. The sunshine is not as bright as it once was. It is, as written in the *I Ching*, "When yang has reached its greatest strength, the dark power of yin is born within its depths, for night begins at midday when yang breaks up and changes into yin." If a further level of consciousness is to be reached, it must be through traversing the dark wood, the lonely space wherein self-examination may begin. It is at this time that Dante needed his Virgil, and when many people in our time seek an analyst, a guide to accompany them on the

difficult journey that lies ahead. It is also at this time that the calling
or the decision to become an analyst may come. For even as it was at
the time of our physical birth, consciousness is born again and again
out of the dark matrix of the unconscious.

The transpersonal stage may emerge out of the introversion brought
about by the crisis that preceded the shift. However, it requires a return
from that introversion, a coming into better balance. It is a time to consider typology. One can no longer use the excuse of the "inferior function" as a way out of addressing difficult tasks. What may once have
been thought of as "inferior" will now be seen as one's "growing edge."
The least developed cognitive mode can be viewed as a challenge to be
taken up. There need be no fear of failure because there is no longer
any attachment to success.

The major task of the transpersonal stage is the transcendence of the
ego. The ego is not discarded, as we may be led to believe when we read
some oriental philosophies—for what they call "ego" incorporates much
of the quality of the persona, as Jung conceived it. The ego that I believe we must transcend, if we would enter the transpersonal stage, is
more like a sense of self-importance. When *this* ego is transcended, our
personal life and our personal problems cease to be the center around
which everything else revolves. We see ourselves in a wider context. We
are part and parcel of the universe, and the universe is also a part of
us. No longer do we cherish the illusion of independence nor seek it
as a goal. We recognize our interdependence upon others, from the person who bakes our bread to the person who formulates the laws under
which we are supposed to live. We know that they influence us, and
that we also and necessarily influence them, for there is no action we
perform that does not have its consequences in the wider world. We
are interacting with the rest of the universe and we know that what we
do affects the totality. This knowledge now begins to guide our behavior.
We act in ways that demonstrate our awareness of mutually influencing
systems.

I believe that when we can truly feel that we are not attached to success, to winning, to helping or to healing, we can begin to be analysts
in the best sense. We no longer need to envision what the path of the
analysand should be. We no longer need to formulate goals, even in
our own minds, that we expect our analysands to achieve. We need only
watch and respond from our own finely-honed intuition to the presen-

tations of the unconscious which, together with conscious intent, constitute the process of the analysand.

There is yet another transition. It falls between the transpersonal stage and the non-personal stage. It is the transition of old age. Our life work has borne the greater part of its fruit and now is the gathering-in time. If the transpersonal stage of life has been lived consciously and conscientiously, old age can also be conscious and meaningful.

A wise man once told me, "if you have as many possessions at sixty as you had at forty, you had better look to your spiritual life." That is something to consider. Meditation takes time and space and emptiness. These three make meditation possible. Letting go also makes it possible to find joy in simple things you didn't notice before. Patterns of light on the wall. Birds half hidden in the branches of a tree. Differences in shape between leaf buds and flower buds. Noticing that Nature is proceeding on her way and also letting go of what no longer suits her purpose. And you and I are part of Nature. We are only here in this body for an interval of time in the larger life cycle which includes our being.

It has always seemed to me that Jung gave short shrift to the years when the energy that has been freed up in the second half of life begins to lose steam. There will come a time, gradually for some and suddenly for others, when we just won't want to "do it" anymore. We'll feel that the world is too much with us. We will not be so much interested in how the world sees us, and there's a certain freedom in that. This freedom from the tasks and interests and concerns that preoccupied us in the past has the potentiality for making space in our lives. Space for embracing the spirit; the spirit that has been guiding us all along, when we were too ego-centered to notice.

Old age requires of us that we realize that we can no longer hope to move the world through our own powers, and that we may find more joy in refining the crucible of our own self, and distilling its contents. In a time when the outer light begins to fade, we need to attend to the fire from within. And, when there will be nothing left but glowing embers, we will need to make preparation for entering into the mystery of the dark.

Among our later tasks are those that involve taking care of unfinished business. Getting in touch with the people to whom we have something to say, but have put it off. Mending broken relationships. Repairing damaged impressions we have left. Saying what we have needed to get off our chests. Telling the truth, with no reservations. Seeing to it that our business affairs are in order. Making provision for the end of life, so that others will not have to decide for us what is to be done. We may even have the privilege of choosing our own death — for that may be one of the blessings of this level of consciousness. Death, I believe, should be the finishing stroke on the canvas of our lives, for when life is an art, something of value is left behind.

A splendid example of how an analyst could meet death was provided by Dr. Esther Harding. She was, for a time, a mentor of mine, and after her death I was given a picture of her in her last days. The picture is a real treasure. It shows that composed old woman, for she was 82, sitting on a toppled pillar amid the ruins of ancient Greece, a big, broad, black sunhat on her head. Years ago Dr. Harding had written much about Greek mythology in her book *Women's Mysteries* and elsewhere, but she had never been to Greece. She determined to go there, and go she did, visiting the site of the oracle at Delphi. I suspect she could have told the prophetess a thing or two. Then she went on to England, the land of her birth, and saw once more the relatives who were left. Having finished her business, she said to her friend, Bill Kennedy, before she retired for the night, "You know, I really feel irresponsible." She went peacefully to sleep and did not waken.

If birth is not the beginning, then death is not the end. We all go into the dark, but it is not forever. For in that darkness, what was disintegrates, and what will yet be coalesces. In that spirit, I would like to leave you with these lines from T.S. Eliot's "East Coker."

> O dark dark dark. They all go into the dark,
> The vacant interstellar spaces, the vacant into the vacant
> I said to my soul, be still, and let the dark come upon you
> Which shall be the darkness of God. As, in a theatre,
> The lights are extinguished, for the scene to be changed
> With a hollow rumble of wings, with a movement of darkness
> on darkness. (Eliot 1943, p.27)

References

Eliot, T.S. (1943). *Four Quartets*. New York: Harcourt, Brace & World.

Ginzberg, Louis, *The Legends of the Jews*, vol.1, Henrietta Szold, trans. Philadelphia: The Jewish Publication Society, 1947, pp.55-59.

Harding, M.E. (1971). *Woman's Mysteries*. New York: G.P. Putnam's Sons.

Isaacs, Jennifer, (ed) *Australian Dreaming: 40,000 Years of Aboriginal History*. Sydney: Lansdowne Press, 1980.

Jung, C.G. (1969). "Stages of Life." *Collected Works*. Vol. 8. Princeton, N.J.: Princeton University Press.

Webster's *Third New International Dictionary, Unabridged*. (1961). Springfield, Mass.: C. & C. Meriam.

Wilhelm. R. and Baynes, C., trans. (1976). *I Ching*. Princeton, N.J.: Princeton University Press.

Wordsworth, W. (1981). Ode. "Intimations of immortality." *Oxford Book of English Verse*, Sir Arthur Quiller-Couch, ed. Oxford: Oxford University Press.

5

Jungian Analysis:

The Impossible Profession

Thomas B. Kirsch, M.D.

In planning this short paper, I wondered what could be said which might be of general value. One of the themes that first interested me was how our lives as analysts blend in with our personal lives, as well as how we as analysts relate to the non-analytic world around us. A second and more personal theme was about what it was like growing up as the child of two first-generation Jungian analysts. I have been reluctant to talk about this in any depth, but upon reflection I realize that it is in fact something I have wanted to share with my professional colleagues for a long time. As a result, a comparison of then and now is going to be the major theme of this paper.

I would like to begin with a few relevant facts about my own childhood. First, my parents both had their primary analysis with Jung and Toni Wolff, and both are and were pioneers in the Jungian world. My father was one of the original analysts in Berlin, Tel Aviv, London, and Los Angeles. My mother began her analytic practice in London when Jung referred her first client to her while she was still nursing me. That client is someone whom I have known in adulthood, and we have discussed what it was like to come for analysis when the analyst was so much into the mothering function. She worked at home, and the boundary between her personal and professional life was fuzzy; in those days the frame had different parameters than what is common today, as there was in general much less of a distance between an analyst's professional and personal life. One wonders how an analysis could take place in such an atmosphere; however, this client has spoken about how much the therapy/analysis helped at the time. It was interrupted by World War Two, when my parents, fearing Hitler's threatened invasion of England, suddenly left and settled in Los Angeles. One can imagine the criticism an analyst would face today if he were to leave his practice on such short notice. In addition, I think that my parents' sudden departure also had a strong impact on their feelings toward Jung. They left with unresolved transferences to him, and no way to resolve them, so their image of Jung remained to a certain extent over-idealized.

In the winter of 1940, Los Angeles—sprawling, arid and dominated by the movie industry—had a very weak sense of itself as a city. My parents, along with the Zellers, founded a small group of devoted followers of Jung. I remember that they continued the pattern of mixing analysis and social relationships. Both of my parents followed the European practice of working at home, and when I came home from school I would knock on my mother's office door to announce my return. I always had an exchange with her patient, while my mother asked about my school. Sometimes my mother would come out and make a snack for me. Over the years, I cannot tell you how many times I have been told, "I remember how you used to come and say hello after school. It was so cute!" My mother would tell her patients a lot about me. On the one hand, I basked in the spillover of the positive transference, but it also made me feel that I had to live up to some idealized expectations. I was the child of parents who had been analyzed, and therefore I was not supposed to have the usual pains of growing up.

The pattern of commingling continued until I left for college; I still experience fallout from these years. A friend of mine from high school visited me recently, and he still remembers meeting a movie star in the dining room, which my parents shared as a waiting room. One event sticks out in my mind as paradigmatic. As a school project I was asked to write a description of my family. I described my mother as a psychologist who doubled as a mother. When I brought this home to her, she had hurt feelings because I saw her primarily as a psychologist and only secondarily as a mother. In actuality, my mother was extremely conscientious in her parental duties; in fact, if anything she was too overprotective and indulgent as a mother. As I look back on that experience, dating from when I was twelve or thirteen, I realize that my unconscious picked up on the strength of her devotion to Jung and analytical psychology, and that everything else was not quite equal in importance, including family life. It was a statement that the professional aspect was central in their lives, and one could say they were consumed by it. Later I will come back to the issue of being obsessed by our work. It is still a major issue for all of us.

In all fairness, to be a Jungian in the 40's and 50's was really esoteric, and my parents received much hostility from many quarters, including psychoanalysts, their neighbors, and the parents of my friends. Since Jung had such a powerful effect upon those around him, it is not surprising that this occurred; a strong over-idealization of Jung affected my parents and many of the first-generation analysts. While to the general public psychoanalysis was only barely acceptable, Jung was really "off." Jung's books, those which had been translated, were always in the metaphysics section of bookstores rather than in psychology. Also, in this era Jung's *supposed* activities and connections with the Nazis was a hot issue, one which has not gone away today. The worst of this was the assumption that Jung was anti-semitic. Jung had a particularly bad name within the culturally Jewish part of Los Angeles, and while I was growing up my parents had to refute this. Psychoanalysts would not speak to my parents on this ground alone. If my father spoke in public, psychoanalysts would walk out because of Jung's alleged anti-semitism. The effect upon me was that I shared my parents' dislike of psychoanalysts.

As Jung was such a strong presence in our family, it was only thought natural that we children should pursue a career connected with analysis. It was impossible for children of that generation of Jungians to be neutral about Jung. One either bore the banner, so to speak, or developed a strong aversion for anything to do with Jung. You can see what path I have taken! These feelings were consciously and unconsciously transmitted to the clients of my parents and the clients' children, who were also expected to have something to do with analytical psychology. I have seen many of these children as adults, with whom I frequently have worked to unravel the difference between the two generations.

I used to wonder how, with all these heavy expectations, I would ever be able to become a Jungian analyst. I basically accepted the Jungian *Weltanschauung*. But in order to find my own way, I had to leave Los Angeles, where it would have been impossible for me to obtain a proper analysis free of my parents, and I needed one. I was fortunate in ending up in San Francisco, which was just far enough away both physically and psychologically. When I first entered the Jungian field, it gave me "name recognition," as one would say in politics. It was not always positive, I might add!! At first, when I had the occasional referral of a patient from my parents, particularly if these were children of their clients who came to the Bay Area as students, I had great difficulty in being objective. But as I have developed my own identity in the Jungian world, the question of being independent of my parents has become less of an issue. I recognized that I could not be completely free from their heritage, even if I had wanted to, which I still do not. But in order to distance myself from their influence, I have been attracted to non-Jungian attitudes, both professionally and personally. This was apparent to me on a recent trip to Portland, Oregon, where I encountered former patients of my parents and did not feel that I had to identify with them. Also, it has become clear to me that typologically I am extraverted intuitive feeling. In the early days, Jo Wheelwright notwithstanding, it was not valued to be an extravert, and I had a great deal of difficulty finding my own true nature. My typology has involved me in the " politics" of Jungian organizations, where I seem to be especially comfortable in a way my parents never were, and where I have in a sense diverged from the world of most first-generation analysts.

In regards to how my experience of growing up in this household affected my practice — first of all, it was important to my parents that I acquire a proper education. My mother had no academic training beyond high school, and my father had a medical degree from Germany, which was of no use to him in California. I saw how this isolated them from the rest of the psychotherapeutic community, and I was and am allergic to that kind of closed group with which they surrounded themselves. Although I am Jungian to the core, I genuinely like interaction and dialogue with others in psychology who are not Jungian.

Secondly, when I started my practice it was important for me to have an office away from home. I wanted and needed to have my personal and professional lives separated. Mixing the two seemed to work for the first generation analysts, but I needed the separation in order not to let myself be consumed by the work. Thirdly, I have tried not to let too many evenings be swallowed up by Jungian activities. Following the example of Jung, my parents would conduct ongoing seminars for interested analysts-in-training and other analysts and analysands. The difference was that my parents had these seminars in the evenings, after a full day of seeing patients. It left precious little time for other aspects of life. Although I recoil at the amount of energy which went into their work, I miss the kind of community feeling and intellectual stimulation which arose out of those seminars. Growing up, I was curious and would go in and see who was there.

My extraverted nature has also expressed itself in how I am as an analyst. I tend to connect dream experiences to the outer life of my patients, rather than primarily interpret them on the inner level. Both levels of interpretation are essential; however, many times I see a relationship to their outer lives which they have not seen. Also, I have found that dream amplification in the traditional Jungian sense does not suit me. Instead, I look for the amplifications in everyday culture. Another area of difference is my emphasis on transference and countertransference phenomena, and especially in the discussion and interpretation of them with patients. The first-generation analysts were quite aware of the transference phenomenon, but on the whole they tended to be less interested in its interpretation except when it got in the way. Finally, as I have better understood my extraverted feeling nature, I have realized that I am no longer the avid reader I once was, so that I do not have the scholarship of many of the first generation. All these changes have emerged slowly and painfully over many years, and they continue to do so.

As I review my childhood from this perspective, I turn to the next generation and wonder how it is for us, with our children. Would we want them to experience analysis? Of what kind? Archetypal? Developmental? Middle-of-the-road? Would we like to see our children grow up to be analysts? I'd like my children to be open to the unconscious and would like them to be interested in their dreams. I and my wife, Jean, who is also a Jungian analyst, try hard not to talk too much about what's going on at the Institute in front of the children. They do not know who my patients are and show little inclination to want to know. However, sometimes professional issues have come up around dinner, but from my point of view the children exaggerate the frequency of such discussions. I am reminded of a small paper by Jim Whitney, an early

San Francisco analyst, whose parents were both analysts. He discusses hearing about the *anima* and *animus* and the *shadow* at the dinner table, but I am careful that my children do not hear any of these Jungian terms in our ordinary conversation.

My parents were dedicated and consumed by their work. These early Jungians really had a "calling" to become analysts, and that calling tended to become all-consuming. Today, it tends to be more of a profession that we put away at the end of our work day. Or is it? There are more and more meetings and conferences. Much energy is spent deciding which ones to go to, and, which ones can be reluctantly given up. If one is not careful, one can go to meetings and serve on professional committees endlessly. I wonder why we have all these conferences and committees? Sure, as professional organizations grow, more structure is required. However, I think we are all looking to get out of the confinement and isolation of our offices and the devouring aspects of being analysts. We are looking to other activities besides eyeballing our patients and having them do likewise. I marvel at the older analysts who have been doing this work for forty and fifty years.

Many of us are hoping to pursue interests and hobbies that connect us with the concrete and tangible in order to counteract the vagueness of the analytic process. In San Francisco many analysts are involved in some form of body work for themselves. Personally, I find that hobbies are an absolute lifesaver. At first I felt extremely guilty for the amount of time and the passion I had for my hobbies. I could spend absolutely endless hours poring over my stamp collection or looking at the latest stereo equipment.

A topic of much discussion and interpretation in my analysis is why I spend so much time on my hobbies. One day I saw an article in one of my stamp magazines by Karl Menninger. He wrote about how important and healthy it is to have a hobby, and his words came at an important time for me. Today I am more accepting of the fact that these outside interests are essential in counteracting too much analytical work. It is generally more important for me to pursue those interests than to read the latest in the Jungian literature or other psychological literature. My concern is that I do not become consumed by the work, and that I live according to my own psychological type.

A recent dream of mine seems to touch on this subject. In the dream I am a visiting doctor on a psychiatric ward. It is very expensive for patients. I want to leave the ward, yet I am curious to see what kind of patient can afford to stay there. I am listening to some classical music which I recognize from a recording. Then, there is a question of my having cancer. It is treatable or not? I seem physically all right. I awaken anxious.

My associations emphasize the expense of analysis and the question of my having cancer. Beyond the personal associations to cancer, I interpreted the cancer as too much analytic work. Can one ever leave it, or does one become consumed by it like a cancer? I love classical music, and this is one important way I separate myself from analysis and the unconscious. My interest in the music is pulling me away from the psychiatric ward in a healthy way.

In the writing of this paper a further issue has presented itself to me quite strongly. One hears today how much we know about transference and counter-transference, and we do. My parents' generation was not as knowledgeable and precise about the subtleties of the analytic process. It is easy to pass judgment on some of the big mistakes they made in the handling of the transference, especially as I have described here. Today we are more and more conscious of the pitfalls of acting out the transference-countertransference. It has been a most necessary swing of the pendulum away from the earlier generation's lack of emphasis on this question. The first-generation Jungians emphasized the teleological aspects of analysis and were less interested in specific ramifications of transference interpretations. My concern today is that we spend so much energy on making every aspect of the transference crystal clear that we lose the connection to the deep unconscious, which is so vital. I am not in favor of the mixed social and professional relationships of former years. The recent concern on ethical issues in analysis is most important. However, I wonder if the pendulum has not swung over too much in the other direction; after all, many patients from that first generation of analysts, including myself, were helped enormously.

6

The Impact of Suffering and Self-Disclosure on the Life of the Analyst

J. Marvin Spiegelman

My theme is that the topics of suffering and self-disclosure are not only central in analytic work, but that they are intermingled and constitute the basis of the strangeness and particularity of our profession.

Patients come to us with their pain and their secrets. As they reveal the sources and concomitants of this suffering, we are willy-nilly drawn in, since our own psyches are affected. The deeper we work, the more is our involvement archetypal and the more, too, is our own suffering included. This occurs by both induction and by commonality of complexes; it constitutes a central dilemma faced by analysts. The Self (with a capital S) is gradually revealed, and our own Selves are also disclosed. We can work on this internally, or share the experience with the patient, or both, but ours is a unique profession in which there is an essentially powerless encounter with suffering wherein healing occurs by the same activated Self-disclosure.

In this, we differ from all sorts of other healers or ministers of the soul. But we are always faced with a dilemma of how much and what to disclose of ourselves and our reactions. The analyst's revelation of personal facts or history is usually of little importance, but sometimes valu-

71

able. It may, however, be merely evasive. What needs to be disclosed, I think, is our honest reaction to the patient before us, what is going on in the background in the way of thought and feeling and fantasy. But this, too, can be evasive or narcissistic or wrong. Thus each patient and each transference is unique. My own resolution, which I call "mutual process," is only one solution; there are others.

This paper consists of an exploration of the themes of suffering and self-disclosure in eight areas, followed by a discussion of an archetypal basis, a mythology, which underlies the themes.

The eight fields are: anxiety, depression, aggression, sexuality, money, alienation, community, and religion. The summaries follow.

Anxiety

"Anxiety Reaction" is the most common diagnosis of patients that we provide insurance companies. It is the least damning, the most general experience of pain. For us, anxiety or dread is the emotion one has when facing the gods, the archetypes. We help by encouraging the encounter with the repressed and rejected. But, in so doing, we are drawn in, we are induced, we too are made anxious. We must then demonstrate how we can deal with this experience. What Jungians have, uniquely, is a capacity to submit to the higher power, to engage the Self with both dignity and fear, along with a realization of both our power and our weakness. We thereby help the patient to do the same. In so doing, the Self of both patient and therapist is revealed. This makes us strange, since we are neither behavior modifiers, who want to get rid of the noxious emotion, nor priests who submit to God, but we do both. We can also find our way with the patient in the maze of the psyche itself. That conscious co-participation in the "emotional plague," as Reich called it, makes us strange, indeed.

Depression

Depression is the most frequent psychopathology of therapists: the suicide rate of psychiatrists is tops. Why? By induction, I believe, we take in the poisons, view the darkness, activate our own. We, like everyone, try to get of it by activity and denial: we jog and swim, and we keep the patient and his darkness at bay. But we cannot; we care too much, and even if we do not, the darkness seeps in and makes us rigid and detached. So we are forced to work some more. Our colleague Bosnak has shown us that Freud's Irma dream, wherein the *anima* is sick, diseased and utterly mistreated by us, reveals us as failures and incompetents. I would add that we are not only depressed by that true reductiveness and limitation, but we are also inspired by our Jungian-type *animae* which are mediumistic and loving. This helps us find our own depth and emotional truth.

We help ourselves and patients in both ways: by dissolving the darkness in activity and evasion; and by deepening through active imagination and acceptance. But we are full of darkness anyway. How do analysts solve it? I do by embracing the simple life. To balance the suffering of the work and our endless complexity, like Freud and Jung, I embrace the simple life of work and love.

Aggression

We move, as a psychologist might be expected to, from depression to aggression, from a darkness drawing us down, to the need to be active, to combat. But we are restrained, we cannot act out. Worse than that, we are endlessly alert, endlessly focussed on the "other." Our work is *contra naturam* and its chief victim is our body, which is restrained from much activity and spontaneity. Although we try to include these impulses in word and image, the body suffers; muscular tension is our disease. We become rigid. Not only that, but the poisons of the unconscious and unexpressed crawl into us, from below and behind, and we metabolize this only partially. We do what we can: Reichian therapy, running and swimming, body work, going into Nature and letting the Great Mother heal us. I also express the aggression in word and image as much I can in the analytic process itself. All of this helps, but only partially. The price of focussing on the psyche and the "other person's" psyche lies in the pain of the body. The "wounded healer," for me, resides in tense muscles.

Sexuality

What was said about aggression is true, too, for sexuality. If Mars is constrained in analytic work, so is Aphrodite. We are stirred up and made lustful, but are enjoined against "acting out." Eros, the spiritualization of relationship, is what we serve, and we endlessly struggle with what and how to accept, include, interpret and deal with the passions of soul and flesh as they arise.

My own resolution of the dilemma of what to reveal is not only to be open about the stimulation and arousal, but also to offer my accompanying fantasies, with the intention of inviting the patient to attend and express his/her own reaction and fantasies. My view of mutual process rests on the belief that body reactions—including sexuality and aggression—are archetypal, if I show ways of dealing with them, by example, I aid integration and wholeness. I imagine that I sit there, with my left hand in touch with the taboo of sexuality and aggression, energy and fantasy, while my right hand keeps connection and care, parenting, morality. I sit in the middle, moving left and right, aiming at wholeness, both within myself and between us. The splits engendered in the work are engaged and healed. Without a religious attitude, I could not do this.

Money

Money is as much filled with affect and taboo as are aggression and sexuality. Deep down, patients usually feel that we, the "Dr. Christians of the soul," ought to make up for the deprivations and injustices of family and world and life and take care of them, for love alone. We hate this. But we (or is it only I?) also believe that we are agents of the Self, that if we serve the Self, then God ought to provide us with enough patients and money to take care of our basic needs. So if they don't pay or even acknowledge our just expectations, murderous thoughts arise: they are destroying our "vocation."

I am reminded of a dream I had some years ago: I am walking across a Renaissance bridge to a futuristic city when a crippled beggar, bodiless and seated on a sort of skateboard, comes to me and announces that he is God. I nod and offer to buy him a drink at a kiosk there. As I acknowledge him, he grows a body and becomes quite whole. We toast each other with wine and he then holds out his palms to me, from which flow a great number of gold and silver coins of every country and time. End of dream.

I understand the dream as a statement about money and God. The Self is both a beggar and provider; it wants to incarnate into my life and needs my recognition. When I do so, and share a relationship of spirit, then all the values and achievements of the ages—the expression of the divine in history—are vouchsafed me. But I can never forget that God is beggar as well as giver and that I, as a carrier of such an everincarnating content, am also beggar and giver. This, too, is my pleasure and my suffering.

Alienation

This word was popular in the fifties, when intellectuals also valued the person who was different from the crowd, the non-organization man. Nowadays almost everybody feels alone in a hostile world, and community is valued, longed for.

We therapists, however, were always alienated—we were once even called "alienists." The one who studies the "sick" mind must be strange; shamans have few friends. It is the individuation process that does this, and we, having embarked on that alchemical path consciously, are endlessly finding our way deep into the inner collective and again outward to the world. But we are peculiar, just because of the play of secrets, reflection, and self-disclosure.

Community

The alienation we suffer leads us directly to the problem of community. We Jungian analysts are part of a "village for people who could not remain in the village." We quarrel and split into factions just like any political collective does, despite the fact that we have a penchant for integrating the shadow. Even our local graduates emerge from training with the feeling that they might be better off not being in our Society at all! This helps individuation, of course, but keeps us like Jung's image of "ships passing in the night." We keep to our inner process and to a few close people, but we lack the skills, capacity, or even the desire to be part of larger communities, even our own. Perhaps we need to discover a kind of alchemical vessel in group work, such as Society meetings, which would both promote our capacities for group life and enhance our individuality. Not group therapy, nor sensitivity training, nor lectures, nor brawls, but something else. In any case, we who were led to the Jungians because we were not very good at staying "in the village," have discovered that the village we have joined is hardly a village at all!

Religion

The step from the issue of community to that of religion is a short one. We analysts are loners, as little likely to be members of a religious congregation as to be active in our community. We are as non-observant as agnostics, yet as religious as devoted practitioners. Our discrepancy militates against membership, but we are just as needy of ritual and communion as the next man. Some of us think that Jungian psychology is the "new dispensation," and some of us think it well to "stand alone." But we all suffer this discrepancy because of the natural human need to be part of a worshipful collective. My own resolution of this suffering has been to form little collectives of my own, and to honor the chief holidays of my own tradition. I am blessed, but it is not enough.

The same week that I dreamed about the Self as a crippled beggar, another dream came to me in which I was informed that God's body constituted the entire universe, that it was like a worm biting its own tail, that its organs were composed of all the galactic systems and planets, and that all living things were cells in this Being. I was further informed that this Being breathed in and out, in a vast harmony, and that those cells (or beings) lucky enough to be located at the places where this breathing occurred had mystical experiences.

My dream said nothing new about the divine; it has been noted generally that we all are One and that God is One in that multiplicity of existence. Yet the difference was that I dreamed it, it happened to me personally. It also compensates the more personal image of God that was in my dream earlier in the week. My dreams reveals the One and the Many, the personal and the transpersonal, but they say nothing about how this is to lived. That, I suppose, is what my life, and life generally, is all about.

Discussion

The foregoing reflections have revolved around the two themes of suffering and self-disclosure. To round out our discussion, I think it is valuable to see these issue from an archetypal perspective provided in myth. I have selected the relation of Teiresias with the Goddess Athena for the theme of nakedness and self-disclosure.

Teiresias, it may be remembered, was a unique prophet and visionary. He warned about the violation of the incest taboo, for example, among other aspects of the Oedipus story. His visionary capacity was gained by him as a consequence of inadvertently glimpsing Athena unclothed. The Goddess of culture and consciousness, born out of the head of Zeus, was deeply offended at being seen naked by this mortal, and blinded him. Remorseful, she recompensed him by giving him inner vision and the capacity to hear the Gods. Teiresias had previously been the unintentional party to another event, when he chanced to see two snakes coupling. Attacked by them, he slew the female and was turned into a woman. He lived as a harlot for seven years, and again saw snakes coupling. Attacked once more, this time he slew the male and he thereby resumed his masculinity.

Our seer "saw things one does not normally see" and was thus punished and honored. We, like Teiresias, see the secrets which lie behind civilization and the advancement of consciousness, and are thus blinded to the outer world as others see and experience it. In recompense, we have increased powers of intuition, and we can see into the depths.

We also see the union of snakes—a symbol of divine healing—and more than most people we are compelled to experience our inner opposites, male and female, most deeply. In this we serve the divine in a feminine aspect, the expansion of consciousness and the advancement of civilization. Like Teiresias, this occurs to us not because of any special merit on our part, but just because we happen to "be there" where secrets of divine and mortal nature are revealed. There is a certain dignity to this, because Athena, and even Zeus and Hera, honored our spiritual forebear. Was it not a prelude to marriage counseling when Zeus and Hera asked Teiresias who had more pleasure in sex, the male or female? We can conclude that the gods are ambivalent about us, wanting us to see, but punishing us. The Self is incarnated in our work, disclosed, and the aim, as Athena supports, is the advancement of consciousness. We are honored and punished thereby.

This leads to the second theme, that of suffering. The archetypal basis I propose in approaching this theme comes from a dream I had early in my first analysis, at Christmas-time in 1950. In it, a divine child was being born, and attended by three new wise men, but these were now a Jewish rabbi, a Christian priest, and a Buddhist priest. This birth and development of the *anthropos* has surely been a theme in my analytic life and is deeply connected to the theme of suffering.

The Christian image of the crucifixion of Christ is centrally concerned with the suffering of God and man as the Self enters into the human condition. The central tenet in Buddhism, *Duhkha*, the condition of suffering or dis-ease, is overcome by an eight-fold path of right living, leading to the experience of the Self. Finally, Judaism, while not espousing suffering as the way to the divine, has certainly been recipient of it throughout its entire history.

My dream and vision of thirty-five years ago surely has mirrored my fate: to cope with the suffering of my patients and myself as this ecumenical birth of the *anthropos* is ushered in at the end of the Piscean age. All three views—the incarnation of divine, the endurance and transcendence of the opposites, and the relationship with God as both a personal and communal fact, have permeated my own analytical work. I suspect that many colleagues have felt the same.

It may be no surprise, then, when I invoke Teiresias and Prometheus, Jesus and Buddha, as guides for our endeavors. It may also not be a surprise when I recall the tradition in Judaism that there are, at one time on earth, twenty-four "just men," *melamed vovnikim*, who must specially suffer because they carry the burden of the godhead. I see the present generations as ones carrying such a burden in increasing numbers, as we are party to the realization that mortals are part of the vast evolutionary process of co-creation of the universe. It is no wonder, then, that we are so uplifted and burdened by what goes on in the ordinary little rooms in which we conduct our analytic work.

S I G O   P R E S S

SIGO PRESS publishes books in psychology
which continue the work of C.G. Jung, the great
Swiss psychoanalyst and founder of analytical
psychology. Each season SIGO brings out a small
but distinctive list of titles intended to make a
lasting contribution to psychology and human
thought. These books are invaluable reading for
Jungians, psychologists, students and scholars
and provide enrichment and insight to general
readers as well. In the Jungian Classics Series,
well-known Jungian works are brought back into
print in popular editions.

Other Titles from Sigo Press

The Unholy Bible *by June Singer*
$32.00 cloth, $15.95 paper

Emotional Child Abuse *by Joel Covitz*
$24.95 cloth, $13.95 paper

Dreams of a Woman *by Shelia Moon*
$27.50 cloth, $13.95 paper

Androgyny *by June Singer*
$24.95 cloth, $14.95 paper

The Dream-The Vision of the Night *by Max Zeller*
$21.95 cloth, $14.95 paper

Sandplay Studies *by Bradway et al.*
$27.50 cloth, $18.95 paper

Symbols Come Alive in the Sand *by Evelyn Dundas*
$14.95 paper

Inner World of Childhood *by Frances G. Wickes*
$27.50 cloth, $14.95 paper

Inner World of Man *by Frances G. Wickes*
$27.50 cloth, $14.95 paper

Inner World of Choice *by Frances G. Wickes*
$27.50 cloth, $14.95 paper

Available from SIGO PRESS, 25 New Chardon Street, #8748A, Boston, Massachusetts, 02114. tel. (508) 526-7064

In England: Element Books, Ltd., Longmead, Shaftesbury, Dorset, SP7 8PL. tel. (0747) 51339, Shaftesbury.